EIGHT PERSPECTIVES ON
PROSPERITY ECONOMICS

Also published by the Prosperity Economics Movement:

Live Your Life Insurance: Surprising Strategies to Build Lifelong Prosperity with Your Whole Life Policy
(Available on Amazon.com or LiveYourLifeInsurance.com)

Busting the Life Insurance Lies: 38 Myths and Misconceptions That Sabotage Your Wealth
(Available on Amazon.com or ProsperityPeaks.com)

Busting the Financial Planning Lies: Learn to Use Prosperity Economics to Build Sustainable Wealth
(Available on Amazon.com or ProsperityPeaks.com)

Busting the Retirement Lies: Living with Passion, Purpose, and Abundance Throughout Our Lives
(Available on Amazon.com or ProsperityPeaks.com)

Financial Planning Has Failed: Reject Typical Financial Advice and Create Sustainable Wealth—Without Wall Street Risks!
(You can download this book for free at ProsperityPeaks.com/Financial… our gift to you in appreciation of your purchase of this book.)

And coming soon:

Busting the Mutual Fund Lies

EIGHT PERSPECTIVES ON PROSPERITY ECONOMICS

Brian Engel • Steve Minnich • Marilyn Johnson • Jim Kindred
Anthony J. Faso • Gina Wells • John Householder • Will Duffy

Introduction by
Kim D. H. Butler

prosperityeconomicsmovement

Eight Perspectives on Prosperity Economics
Copyright © 2017 Prosperity Economics Movement

ISBN: 978-0-9913054-2-1

First Print Edition
July 2017

Produced in the United States of America

Prosperity Economics Movement
22790 Highway 259 South
Mount Enterprise, TX 75681
www.ProsperityPeaks.com

DISCLAIMER: Although the authors and publisher have made every effort to ensure that the information in this book was correct at press time, the authors and publisher do not assume and hereby disclaim any liability to any party for any loss, damage, or disruption caused by errors or omissions, whether such errors or omissions result from negligence, accident, or any other cause. This book is also not intended to provide specific financial or legal advice. The authors and publisher do not assume and hereby disclaim any liability to any party for any loss, damage, or disruption caused by the information in this book. For advice and guidance specific to your situation, please contact Prosperity Economics Movement or a qualified expert. If you do not agree to these terms, you may return this book to Prosperity Economics Movement for a full refund.

TRADEMARK NOTICE: Prosperity Economics, Prosperity Economic Advisor, and Prosperity Economic Advisors are trademarks of Prosperity Economics Movement.

This book was published with the guidance and services of Social Motion Publishing, a benefit corporation that specializes in social-impact books. For more information, go to SocialMotionPublishing.com.

Contents

Introduction—Kim D. H. Butler
Typical Financial Planning: Are You Caught in the Matrix? vii

Chapter 1—Brian Engel
Apples to Oranges: Comparing Qualified Retirement Plans
to Whole Life Policies 1

Chapter 2—Steve Minnich
The Twisted Tale of Three Pigs: A Parable About Your Money 11

Chapter 3—Marilyn Johnson
The Secret Sauce: Blending Nonfinancial Assets
to Create, Grow, and Preserve Your Family's Legacy 21

Chapter 4—Jim Kindred
What Your Banker Won't Tell You: Keys to the Bank
for Small Business Owners 33

Chapter 5—Anthony J. Faso
I Kid You Not: Why You Should Place a Life Insurance
Policy on Your Child 43

Chapter 6—Gina Wells
A Balancing Act: Using Leverage to Build
Your Financial Nest Egg 53

Chapter 7—John Householder
Make No Mistake: How to Pay for College
Without Breaking the Family Bank 65

Chapter 8—Will Duffy
The Other Side of the Coin: Compound Interest—
Financial Truths to Protect Your Wealth 77

About the Prosperity Economics Movement 87

Consulting a Prosperity Economics Advisor 92

Book a Prosperity Economics Advisor for Your Next Event 93

Order this book 96

Kim D. H. Butler

Introduction

Typical Financial Planning: Are You Caught in the Matrix?

In the 1999 hit film *The Matrix*, the main character, Neo, discovers that modern life as we know it is an illusion. It serves to keep the masses satisfied and sedated while the evil forces behind the illusion go about their nefarious ways.

This is an apt metaphor for typical financial planning in the United States today. The mainstream financial industry and media have sold most of us on an illusion—that the way to prosperity is through an array of investment vehicles that are typically tax deferred and employer based. And it's an easy process: Sign a form or two, and a chunk of money will automatically be deducted from your paycheck and deposited into your 401(k) or similar plan. Better yet, your employer will likely match a percentage of your contribution. It's such a smooth and seamless system that the vast majority of people never question it. Like the population living "in the matrix," we go about our days happy in the belief that we are secure and in control. But the truth is far from idyllic.

In reality, typical financial planning is built around the needs of Wall Street and the US government. Our benefit—the potential of security and comfort in retirement—is a mere byproduct. This is not to say a 401(k) or IRA is a bad thing; any retirement plan is better than no plan. But these are not the glorious roads to prosperity they are usually portrayed to be. If you want to be financially prosperous, not just safe or comfortable, then you need to understand what prosperous people do with their money. The problem is, the guy yelling about stocks on cable TV isn't telling you what that is.

Fortunately, over the past decade or so, a growing number of financial advisors are rediscovering a set of principles that the wealthy have been using for decades to achieve true prosperity. These principles, which long predate the typical financial advice of today and cover more than just retirement plans, make up the foundation of what we call Prosperity Economics. To support these advisors and principles, I founded a nonprofit called the Prosperity Economics Movement.

In the pages of this book, you will meet eight leading advisors in the Prosperity Economics Movement. Each will offer their perspective on a particular aspect of finance, ranging from qualified plans to small business ownership, college savings to compound interest, and more. You will discover that many of the financial truths you've been taught, and have come to accept as reality, aren't necessarily true. Like Neo in *The Matrix*, you will be given a glimpse of a parallel world you didn't realize exists and yet has been all around you.

We truly hope our book will give you at least a few nuggets of information to widen your money perspective—or better yet, totally shift your thinking. As with everything in finance, these tools aren't applicable or ideal for everyone. But if we end up opening your mind to the potential of Prosperity Economics, we encourage you to read the other books we publish for greater detail. And of course, feel free to contact the Prosperity Economics Advisor who referred you to this book or contact our office via ProsperityPeaks.com for personal guidance.

Thank you for reading our book and sharing your valuable time with us.

About the Author

Kim D. H. Butler is helping Americans build wealth... WITHOUT Wall Street risks!

A "typical" financial planner in the 1990s, Kim obtained her Series 7 and 65 licenses and a coveted financial planning certification. But as time passed, she grew frustrated as she realized that many financial planning practices were irrelevant at best, sometimes even misleading or insane! The projections of financial planning gave clients a false sense of security, but no guaranteed results. Money was subjected to unknown future taxes and put under the use and control of others. Worse yet, the system rewarded planners and money managers when they convinced clients to put (and keep) their money at risk!

Today, Kim is president of Partners for Prosperity, a Registered Investment Advisory firm that serves clients in all 50 states, as well as a best-selling author of several books. Along with her husband Todd Langford of Truth Concepts financial software, Kim is also the co-founder of Prosperity Economics Movement, which offers an alternative to "typical" financial planning.

Kim can be reached through Partners4Prosperity.com.

Brian Engel

Chapter 1

Apples to Oranges: Comparing Qualified Retirement Plans to Whole Life Policies

We have all been financially educated (read: manipulated) by many sources. But specifically, the white noise of advertising has made us believe in the false paradigm that qualified plans, such as 401(k)s, are the only smart choice for our retirement savings. To open your mind to options outside the typical financial world view, I am going to compare apples to oranges, or the qualified plan to the whole life insurance plan.

My intention with this chapter is to get your attention—I want you to pay more attention to your money and how it is put to work and used. You will find no numbers here. So for those overwhelmed by numbers, I hope that anxiety will be eased. For those who like and need numbers, my intention is for these concepts to compel you to dig deeper, to really understand what is going on with your money.

THE QUALIFIED PLAN: THE APPLE

Any 401(k), 403(b), or IRA falls under the classification of a qualified plan (QP). So, the following facts are true for all of them when invested in equity vehicles (stocks, mutual funds, etc.), which, in most cases, is all that is on offer. However, are these "tried and true" retirement vehicles really the best place to save for your retirement? Let's see.

Taxes

When participating in a QP, you must remember that you have a partner: the US government. And this partner sets the rules and tax rates. The basic assumption behind a QP is that it allows a saver to defer a higher tax now in order to pay a lower rate in retirement.

But your tax rate is determined by income level and the tax tables minus deductions. With all the recent media attention on the rising national debt, increasing health care costs, and our failing infrastructure, which way do you think tax rates will go—up or down? Second, who really wants to have a lower income in retirement? It may happen to a lot of people, but that should not be their plan. The reality for most that do succeed in saving for retirement is that they will not pay a lower rate. And lastly, the deductions you have early in life will no longer be there. The two biggest for most are children and mortgage interest, but kids leave the nest and mortgages are eventually paid off.

Risk

How many times in your lifetime has the stock market crashed? Risk is a big flaw in a QP. On a total market scale, valuations of stocks and mutual funds can tank, even in good times. Also, the growing and evolving threat of terrorism as well as international conflicts (both economic and martial) have brought concerns of a market or corporate crisis to a new level, with those effects directly impacting market dynamics. The negatives of globalization are not discussed much in the media.

Volatility

This problem plays on our minds throughout our saving years, as we see our account balance ride a roller coaster daily. But the real problem lies when you draw on your QP in retirement. If you need to withdraw that income in a down year, those reduced-value dollars are gone—forever. This is probably the single biggest risk to a person running out of money in retirement.

Restrictions

During accumulation and distribution phases, your partner, the government, has made the rules, and they are not in your favor.

During accumulation, the money you put into the plan is locked up for years, decades. A limited menu of withdrawal options is possible. But even these options should be considered a last resort. And should you decide to remove your money without compliance, through those small holes provided, then you are assessed a penalty. Are you kidding me?

During distribution, if you try to continue deferring the tax to be paid, you will be forced to withdraw anyway. At 70½ years old, it is mandatory to take "required minimum distributions." This is one of the biggest reasons that a lower tax rate at withdrawal is unlikely, if not impossible, for those who have aggressively saved in their QP.

Fees

Fees, fees everywhere, but you may never know how many or how much. Fees in your mutual funds. Fees in your QP. Fees for trading. Fees for moving funds. The list is long and steep. And the SEC does not require them all to be stated.

Most do not realize what effect even the stated fees have on reducing their future balance. Even the low fees of index funds can have a dramatic negative effect. If your money is already trapped inside a 401(k), what can you do about the fees? Well, you can't do anything about tax within the plan, but you can reduce management fees while still maintaining diversity/growth and as much safety as you can get.

I like the strategy of using the low-cost index funds and a cash account in concert. Most 401(k) plans will have at least one of each of these types of funds. With an index fund (S&P as an example), you cover a diverse range of companies and industry sectors. With the money that is already in the plan, you divide it evenly between the index fund and the cash account, and for incoming new money, you divide that also. Then, on a quarterly or annual basis (data shows it makes almost no difference), you rebalance the accounts (make them even). This strategy keeps management fees low and trading commitments at the correct valuations, with a safety cushion of cash that keeps the whole plan afloat if the market goes negative. Both accounts will act as shock absorbers to each other, with safety and market risk/reward balanced. This is a great strategy, and anyone can do it without paying for advice or worrying over decisions.

Average Rate of Return

The entire world of Wall Street advertising is based on average rates of return. But these numbers are misleading, to the point of being outright lies. Why? Because as soon as you introduce a negative number—a down year or period—into a string of numbers to be averaged, the result is meaningless. The only way to know what is really happening is to calculate your actual rate of return on your own balances.

Math Inversion

This is my term for when the math does not add up—or at least is counterintuitive—like with averages. The most glaring example of this is when one of the frequent market crashes occurs. A common misconception is that if a market falls 30 percent, it will recover if it rises 30 percent. The correct answer is the market must rise almost 43 percent to recover lost ground. (Do the math: 100 x .30 = 70; 70 x 1.43 = 101.) Since all rates of return must reference a time frame, "five years to recover" from a crash really means we'll likely need an even greater return and longer time frame to recover.

Rate of Return

Most people assume, and in some cases fervently believe, that the return in their account is somewhere between the stated fund returns and the market at large. By any objective analysis of mutual funds, the returns are not even close to those stated. Most fund managers are not able to sustain returns anywhere near the major indexes. This is not good news for the mutual fund saver who is committed for decades in their QP. In most plans, these funds are the only option, and there is a limited menu at that.

When discussing internal return, we must talk actual return instead of any other measure, like average. It is the only way to see what is going on in your account. And you still must consider what your biggest partner, the government (federal and maybe state), will take from your account when you decide to begin to draw on it.

Lastly, the flow of your money is against you. Yes, deferred dollars go into the plan and you do not pay tax on them . . . yet. But when you draw, you pay on the dollars you put in and the growth of them (let's hope there is some). Then the domino party starts. Those dollars coming out are classified as provisional income. This type of income triggers more tax on the rest of your retirement income, including Social Security.

There Must be a Better Way

Reviewing the QP, we see the full picture of what is on offer. So why are we still convinced to take our savings (and admittedly the deferred-tax portion), put it into an account for decades with limited investment options (whose benefits are largely misstated and inflated), and entrust it with partners who can decide to change the plan in the future? Why would we bare all this risk only to find out much later what the tax bill will be?

There must be a better way. What if there was an account that enabled you to save, not lose, money (plus receive other benefits), while allowing you access to your money throughout your life—without having partners to chip away at the work done?

Well, there is and has been for decades . . . centuries, really:

Participating whole life with a mutual insurance company.

PARTICIPATING WHOLE LIFE—THE ORANGE

So what is this exactly? At its core, it's life insurance. To provide that benefit, the insurance company builds a store of funds over your policy and lifetime, which you pay premiums for. But it's not that simple. Contrary to what you may have been taught about life insurance, with a whole life policy, you actually have access to those funds throughout your life; it grows and receives dividends, and it's flexible, safe, and tax-deferred. (Just make sure you choose a policy that pays dividends; otherwise, any profits earned will stay with the insurance company.) The following are other benefits of investing in whole life with a mutual insurance company.

Tax-Protected

The principal will not be taxed; it already has been. The growth and dividends will be taxed only if you do not follow very simple rules. And when you draw retirement income, it does not trigger the negative effects of provisional income, like your QP does.

Safe

Together, you and your insurance agent pick a vehicle that is time-tested with companies that are bound by regulation and not exposed to wild changes in governance, so we have a very stable and safe place to store wealth as we accumulate it. Century-old companies bound by regulation and contract law with conservative fiscal practices are now your partners.

Contract Law

Because of the history of contract and insurance law, you can have a measure of trust in the guarantees built into this vehicle. These guarantees bestow ownership rights to you that provide protection (death benefit), growth (cash value growth and growth in a death benefit), and income (dividends that can add protection and growth again). That ownership can be thought of as equity in a property—only better, because it keeps growing.

Loan Provision

Most people think that paying cash is the best method for major purchases. However, using the funds built into your policy can be better. Once the funds are in the policy, the power of those funds is never lost. While you use the funds, they keep growing. That is an incredible strength to a lifetime savings tool. Most forget there is a cost to using cash, which is that the future power of that money is gone forever. You lose the interest gain you would have otherwise had. Interest is either paid or given up—always, with no exceptions. So the better path is to accept a small interest cost in order to gain a lifetime of growth and benefit.

Death Benefit

Are there fees in this plan? Yes, in the form of insurance costs. But instead of paying fees whether you win or lose, like you do in your 401(k), you get something in exchange with a life insurance policy, and it comes in the form of a death benefit.

Uninterrupted Compounding

With guaranteed growth, dividends, and safety, you get uninterrupted compounding. This is nearly unattainable in any other vehicle. Any market-based plan has wild fluctuations and negative periods, which will not result in an ever-growing arc.

Flexibility

No matter how much you save—big or small—you can have a policy built for you. We all go through periods of fluctuating cash flow. Our savings plan should be able to react to that. And if we are really low, we should be able to access our money and not go into debt elsewhere.

Multiplier Effect

Your whole life insurance policy can help your QP. Many of us have a qualified plan though work. I am not saying that is bad, especially if your company contributes to the plan via a match. However, I suggest you take the match, but stop there. For most, it is far better to save the excess money elsewhere.

Instead, take that money and put it into your whole life policy.

Later in life, when you are living on those accumulated dollars, you'll have options. Tax consequences, market conditions, and other income sources should all be considered when deciding when to draw from which account. Options give us power—our dollars are multiplied. You also have the legacy and liquidity that the combined plan gives you. Would you rather have a death benefit, a store of cash that continues to grow, and QP funds that were boosted by a match, or just the QP?

The multiplier effect is powerful! You might have more funds in the QP alone, but after taxes, fees, etc., which investment vehicle will give you more spendable, accessible, liquid dollars?

Velocity

This is a foreign concept to most but an important one. Can you save, buy, and retain financial power all with the same dollars? That sounds crazy, right?

With a whole life policy, you can. Imagine you get a $20,000 bonus at work. You need a car. You remember reading about velocity. So, you put the $20,000 into your new whole life policy, borrow against it for the car, and retain the power of that $20,000 for the rest of your life.

You will continue to save, right? Of course. So, you will replace that borrowed $20,000 with future dollars, while the original $20,000 you put in your policy continues to grow. It sounds like smoke and mirrors, but each incremental gain like this over a lifetime is huge.

THE UPSHOT

So, are qualified plans bad? No. The way they have been portrayed is bad, because for so many of us, it is the only and primary savings vehicle for retirement—with all its inherent problems and limitations.

Likely you have one, and that's great. More savings buckets are good. But start a new bucket—one that you have far greater control over and that benefits you in multiple ways—instead of just relying on a retirement savings plan that's loaded with restrictions and fees.

Today, limit the contributions you are making to your 401(k) and only put in what you need to get your full employer match—but no more after that. Put the rest into a savings account you will not raid. Then contact one of the contributors to this book to find out what your next steps should be.

Capture all the benefits you are due for your retirement savings and for the legacy you want to leave to those people and organizations that you care about.

Commit to reading the rest of this book and implementing the concepts and strategies you find here. I hope I've captured your attention and inspired you to make a change that will benefit you for the rest of your life.

About the Author

Brian Engel has had a lifetime of training and education focused on efficiency, simplicity, and result-oriented planning. His path through the U.S. Naval Academy to becoming a Marine Corps officer and tactical pilot led to an outlook closely aligned with the certainty, flexibility, and protection offered by whole life insurance strategies.

Years of mentor-directed self-education led him to a tectonic shift in his thinking towards personal finances. Realizing that everyone could benefit from this paradigm shift, he decided to become a proponent and educator of a whole life-based philosophy and financial life.

Brian can be reached at Ascension Financial: 603-812-1344.

Steve Minnich

Chapter 2

The Twisted Tale of Three Pigs: A Parable About Your Money

Are you looking for a safe and guaranteed way to grow money for your retirement cash flow needs? Would you find it hard to believe that whole life insurance could be exactly what you're looking for?

If you read Chapter 1, you're probably starting to see the bigger picture. In this chapter, I'm going to encourage you to think creatively. But first, you'll need to do something that will always feel uncomfortable. Think about common knowledge vs. uncommon knowledge. Which one makes us feel comfortable? Did Albert Einstein use common or uncommon knowledge?

Uncommon knowledge makes us feel uncomfortable because, when you hold an unpopular or unorthodox belief, there will always be those friends and family who disagree with you—sometimes vehemently. You might even question yourself. But when it comes to growing your retirement fund, the only way you will be successful is if you use uncommon knowledge. In this chapter, I will show you how to use your Financial GLASSES™ to acquire and use that knowledge to your advantage. So, let's get started!

Bye, Bye Pension Manager—Hello, DIY

In 1974, the Employee Retirement Income Security Act (ERISA) was passed. Prior to this, private businesses had professional pension managers. Employees knew from day one what their defined benefit (i.e., "their monthly retirement check") would be. But ERISA set minimum standards for pension plans in private industry. Basically, it established the precedence for the 401(k), 403(b), 457, and IRA plans we now have.

After 1974, instead of having a highly trained and qualified pension manager watching out for your best interests, you had to go it alone. How many of us spent only a few minutes at lunch with our co-workers deciding what investments we would choose to give us the best growth over the next 40 years? Instead of having a predictable future retirement income, we had to do the best we could at amassing a big pile of money that would pay us some unknown interest rate, which was supposed to provide all our retirement needs.

Here's the big thing you need to realize. Employees used to exclusively have defined benefit plans such as pension plans — the payout or distribution was predetermined in the plan design. Now, we mostly have defined contribution plans. When you sign up for a 401(k) or 403(b) or similar tax-qualified plan, your plan design limits how much you can contribute in your principle payments and when. These contribution plans, also known as "qualified" plans, were the best thing that ever happened to . . . Wall Street. Oh, sorry, you thought I was going to say "employees." Nope. Once again, the hard-working individual investor was dumped on by the big boys in the pin-striped suits on Wall Street and in the corporate offices of the investment banking world.

Am I making it too obvious that I don't have much respect for Big Government, Wall Street, and the Federal Reserve Banking System? Politics as usual, crony capitalism, and the greed and corruption found in many of our financial institutions have ruined many plans for a secure retirement.

We tend to learn best when we hear stories. So, to drive home this point in a creative yet engaging way, I present the following parable.

The Twisted Tail of Three Pigs—A Parable About Your Money

Once upon a time there were three little pigs. The youngest pig wanted to make his fortune in the stock market. His straw house investment strategy went up quickly. But it also went down quickly. He liked the excitement of seeing his fortunes bouncing and rebounding. He had the stomach for it.

The middle pig wanted to make his fortune in the real estate market. His stick-built-house investment strategy also went up quickly. It was a bit stronger than his brother's straw house. But it, too, became shaky.

The wise, oldest brother built a house of bricks. His idea was to make predictable growth on smaller investments over a long, long time. The wise, oldest brother's house was big and strong. He continued making wise, long-term investments and eventually had predictable future retirement income.

When the straw and stick houses fell, the younger pigs decided to build a house that looked a lot like their oldest brother's house. Unfortunately, they used a very poor grade of building materials. Even though their brick house looked almost exactly like their wise, oldest brother's home, they knew their cheap house wouldn't last. But they thought, "Why spend so much money building with such expensive materials? We want to make a lot of money—and quickly."

The middle pig brother went into politics. He sold government and municipal bonds from the main floor of his cheap brick house. He raised taxes on the rich and passed all kinds of laws to "help" the poor and middle class. He even passed laws that "helped" the financially illiterate buy their very own stick house (although they couldn't afford even the modest interest-only payments).

The youngest pig brother moved into the cheap brick house with the middle pig. These two younger pigs were very close.

The youngest pig brother went into banking. While the middle pig sold bonds, the youngest pig sold CDs and money market accounts. Both the younger brothers wanted to make as much money as possible. So, they didn't pay their customers very much, but they charged high fees.

In fact, the youngest pig brother was so eager to make more money, he even set up a printing press in the basement. His goal was to print as much money as he could and buy lots of stuff and resell it at a profit. "What a great plan!" he thought.

That was their retirement plan. The two younger brothers kept their straw and stick houses and continued to charge high fees for "helping" their clients. But they did most of their business out of the cheap brick house they had built to look like the wise, oldest pig's wonderful, strong brick house.

So, the three brother pigs lived happily until the Big Bad Wolf came in 2001, and again in 2008. The wise, oldest pig's solid brick house stood against the wolf's terrible, awful huffing and puffing. But the straw and stick houses sadly and quickly came tumbling down.

Since the two younger pigs had political and financial power, and because they were, after all, living together in the same cheap brick house, they decided to help each other. The youngest brother printed even more money.

Billions each month were pumped into the economy. The

youngest pig used all this extra money to buy his politician brother's bonds. Now the politically powerful, middle pig brother could say that he was paying off all his loans. This scheme worked like magic . . . at least until the customers figured out what was going on.

What Does This Parable Mean?

The Twisted Tail of Three Pigs is all about money. Your money. But first, let's take a closer look at the health-conscious, wise, oldest brother pig.

Unlike his portly and gluttonous younger brothers, the wise, oldest pig stayed fit and trim. He was careful about both his physical health and the health of his wealth.

When you're overweight, you might try extreme measures to lose weight. For instance, you could appear to be a few ounces lighter if you removed your glasses. This would also have the added benefit of obscuring the numbers on the scale!

Lots of people are that way about their market investments. They want to set it and forget it. They have better things to do with their time.

But you're not going to do a better job of retirement saving when what you're really doing is risky investing. Can you see that Wall Street has convinced you to trust that your 401(k) plan is well managed and there's nothing to worry about? They say: "Just set it and forget it. Leave the money alone. Buy and hold. You're young and have plenty of time to rebound from a market loss. You haven't lost money until you sell your stocks and mutual funds."

Really? Here's the truth. It's not if you will suffer a market loss but when! You already know that loss is very likely, especially if you stay in the market for any length of time. But didn't your advisor tell you to stay in the market for a very long time, or did I miss something? When you have a market loss, the sad thing is that you not only lose your hard-earned money, but you also lose the time it took to make those gains in the first place. We need to forget this nonsense that we are "saving" for retirement in a "qualified" plan. If your money is in the market—it's at risk! Mutual funds are not a safe and secure investment. They can and will lose value at some point during your working years. Brokers might tell you that you've had average returns of 8.46 percent over the last 18 years, even with four down years. But your actual, compounded returns over this period were just 3.63 percent.

With that said, it is important to set aside money on a regular basis. Having money automatically and electronically withdrawn from your paycheck means you are far more likely to amass a nice chunk of change. But wouldn't you also agree that Wall Street's (and the government's) plan to have you regularly deposit money into their game probably serves to enrich a lot of stock market traders? I do not trust the government's "qualified" retirement plans. They can and have regularly changed the rules while you're still playing the game!

But you're in the government's game, and they set the rules. Think about it: How would you react if I offered to lend you money and said, "You don't have to pay me back right away, but when I do need the money, I'll tell you what the loan's interest rate is and how quickly I want you to pay me back." No financially savvy person would go for that kind of phony loan deal. Yet, we have listened to Wall Street, the government, and our CPA tell us things like: "See how much money I saved on your taxes this year? You'll be in a lower tax bracket when you retire. Tax deferred is the best way to save for retirement! Everyone wants qualified savings, don't you?"

Unless your CPA is a prophet, there's no way they can possibly know what any tax bracket will be when you retire. You could easily be living on less money and still be paying higher taxes.

If you believe (as many do) that tax rates are more likely to be higher in the future, then why are you putting off paying your tax bill until some distant year in the future—and on a larger sum of money? You're not only putting off the tax bill, but you're also putting off the tax calculation!

Remember that phony loan deal? You'd never go for that offer, right? Or would you? Why are you assuming that the government has your best interests in mind? If they really wanted you to keep and save more of your money, why didn't they just lower your tax rate to begin with? Your money doesn't belong to the government, or does it? Whose retirement are you planning anyway—yours or Uncle Sam's?

You've probably figured out on your own that the wise, oldest pig and his brick-house savings strategies have everything to do with creatively using life insurance products. These uniquely designed strategies will grow tax-free and provide tax-free access to your funds to supplement your needs during your retirement years.

Technically, insurance should not be called "savings." However, you would likely agree that getting tax-free growth on your insurance policy cash values and having tax-free access to it (via policy loans, dividends, or partial surrenders), plus the tax-free transfer of this asset to your heirs, is exactly what you want for your "safe money." This strategy of protecting your wealth certainly sounds better than risking your retirement "savings" in the stock market. If nothing else, at least it's a better place to start, even if you decide to risk money in the market.

As the parable says, "The wise, oldest brother built a house of bricks. His idea was to make predictable growth on smaller investments over a long period of time." Admittedly, the eldest brother pig was not always as genuinely concerned about client needs as he is today. Prior to the 1980s, life insurance and annuities were generally unsatisfactory repositories of retirement funds. Enticed by high commissions, insurance agents tended to push product like a used car salesman on a Friday night. But things are different today.

A New Perspective

In the chapters to come, you will learn much more about these creatively designed strategies that enable death-benefit insurance to finally provide living benefits. You'll learn how to set up your own privatized banking-like system and how to redirect back to yourself much of the taxes, fees, and interest that you would normally pay to someone else over a lifetime. You need to know the facts. That way, you will make better financial decisions. You just have to start seeing things in a much different way!

You may think there's a lot of hidden meaning in this altered version of the classic children's story. But it's not really hidden. The problem is we are all so focused on what we have to do every day (just to make a living) that a lot of what goes on in the financial world and in government agencies goes unnoticed. So, what we think is hidden is actually sitting right in front of us, in plain sight! You just have to put on your Financial GLASSES. This stands for:

Guaranteed tax-free growth
Liquidity
Accessibility with accountability
Safety of principal
Secure financial institution managing your tax-free whole life insurance account
Enjoyment
Self-fulfilling

Now that you have your Financial GLASSES on, start carefully observing what's really going on with your financial health and your "wealth health." You should be saving for retirement. Using an automated electronic funds transfer (EFT) to regularly place some of your monthly earnings into your own whole life account will put you on the road to success. Pay your taxes now at a lower rate so your money will:

- Grow tax-free.
- Provide tax-free access.
- Blossom and transfer to your heirs tax-free should you permanently "retire" from this earth sooner than you planned.
- Become self-fulfilling. If you become disabled and are physically unable to work, your whole life insurance account can be set up to fund itself for the rest of your life. It could be designed so your deposits would continue to be made on your behalf, even if you became disabled.

Through your new Financial GLASSES, you will clearly see what is going on around us. And that will make all the difference in your ability to make great financial decisions.

About the Author

Steve Minnich is the founder and president of TrueWealth Financial, host of the popular SmartWealth Radio Show, and an instructor of retirement Boot Camp workshops at local community colleges. He earned his BA in education in 1975 and an MA in instructional communications in 1985. Combining years of teaching experience with creative financial strategies, Steve provides a unique, learning-focused approach to retirement cash flow and income planning. When not teaching clients, Steve enjoys spending time with his grandkids, woodworking, gardening, photography, and hiking the beautiful mountains in Northeastern Washington State. For 26 years, Steve was a musician in an Air National Guard band.

Steve can be reached at steve.minnich@gmail.com.

Marilyn Johnson

Chapter 3

The Secret Sauce: Blending Nonfinancial Assets to Create, Grow, and Preserve Your Family's Legacy

You are working hard and making money to support your lifestyle and your family. And you dream of leaving a legacy that will serve, protect, and support future generations. The challenge is not only enjoying your financial resources today, but also inspiring your family to be good stewards of these resources. You wonder if you will ever have the assets you think you need; whether you can successfully navigate the unpredictable economy and its impact on taxes, health care, and education. And, even then, will your family break the "three strikes and you're out" curse—where your generation makes the money, but by the end of the third generation, it's gone?

With all these thoughts swirling in your mind, you may be surprised to discover that you already have more assets than you realize. And these "hidden" assets are vital to creating, growing, and preserving your financial wealth.

So how do you discover these assets?

When you think of your assets, what comes to mind? If you are like most people, you think of stocks, bonds, your house, your possessions—mostly financial assets. But think again. What is more important to you than money and possessions?

Consider news reports right after a natural disaster. People almost always say, as they are looking through the rubble of their lives after the destruction, "At least I have myself, and my family, and I can rebuild; I can rebuild my life." There may be insurance money, but to rebuild—especially your business or your home—you will need to employ all your nonfinancial assets first: your values, experience, skills, and your network of friends and family. You may even need to take advantage of government or community-based resources, such as disaster relief programs. Let's face it, most of us have many nonfinancial assets but never think about how to grow or protect them.

We work with an advisor to grow and protect our financial assets, but why do we overlook these nonfinancial assets—those we cannot replace and the ones most of us value the most. Shouldn't we broaden the definition of assets to include not just the tangible, but also the intangible ones that typically die with us?

What if you could successfully capitalize the intangible ones, put them to work, and leverage and multiply them? Well you can, and it will create the engine that enables you and your family to successfully transfer all your assets through successive generations.

That's the secret of sustainable wealth: knowing, organizing, harnessing, and nurturing all your assets—both nonfinancial and financial.

So, let's take a closer look at how you can leverage these nonfinancial assets, and let's call them capital as it's helpful to treat them like financial capital. It begins with a shift in your mind-set.

YOUR NONFINANCIAL ASSETS
Human Capital

Talents. Health. Well-Being. Ethics. Morals. Character. Unique Abilities.

Our human assets are at the heart of a sustainable wealth management strategy. Like with financial assets, there are principles and techniques to assist you in capturing them for use today and tomorrow. These assets identify your unique abilities, values, ethics, and morals. They are the core of how you and your family view yourselves. They drive what you do with your money.

The techniques for capturing these assets start with identifying the ones we were born with, ranking them, and placing them in a "repository," often referred to as the "family bank." The bank metaphor is useful, as deposits and withdrawals grow when our human assets take the form of family journals, writings, videos, and recordings—a living record that spans generations.

Intellectual Capital

Life Experiences. Education. Heritage. Traditions. Faith. Networks. Skills. Ideas.

Your intellectual assets are capitalized when your life's experiences, both good and bad, are captured for use by all family members. Think of the value of avoiding costly mistakes or having the knowledge of a more efficient path to success from past and present family. Each family member becomes an engaged participant when their formal education, wisdom, alliances, reputation, and relationships are shared.

The family bank can hold intellectual capital, such as genealogy records and life stories. Family vocational and professional practices, and specialized skills, such as earning college credits in high school and securing venture capital—as well as fitness programs, creative writing, and real estate investing—can be banked, withdrawn, and shared at family reunions.

This family knowledge becomes a powerful tool for how to live a prosperous life, avoid costly mistakes, and enhance the chance of early success.

Social Capital

Values. Purpose. Charitable Gifts. Taxes. Mentoring. Volunteering. Social Entrepreneurship.

Social assets may seem harder to define. Do you consider taxes to be an asset or a liability? Maybe an odd question considering most accountants will put taxes on the liability side, but if no one paid taxes, there would be no societal benefits, such as roads, police and fire protection, medical care, schools, and libraries. So, taxes can be an asset.

The real issue is we don't like giving up choice and control over cash assets when we turn them over to the Treasury. But it is possible to regain choice and control. With family and philanthropic values and entrepreneurial know-how banked, portions of what might otherwise have been paid in taxes can be directed to a cause that you and your family want to support. It becomes a hands-on philanthropic experience. There is a transfer of purpose, values, and practical know-how through the process of learning to give away.

INTEGRATING NONFINANCIAL ASSET STRATEGIES

Integrating nonfinancial asset strategies within the financial planning process has been widely discussed for years, but far less implemented. Let's examine why by first looking at financial assets more closely.

Your financial assets are those tangible assets like your savings, stocks and bonds, 401(k)s, and real estate that you count on to ensure financial independence. Typical financial planners focus only on these assets and emphasize that these alone must take care of you today, as well as your family legacy. The mind-set and strategies reflect limiting ideas of "what you can afford" and how much you must accumulate—a stockpiling mentality.

In contrast, designing a plan that integrates financial and nonfinancial assets provides clarity around family values and purpose, and the focus shifts to "possibilities and opportunities" and a process that creates a more flexible and sustainable way to live. Planning solutions are focused on optimizing all the family assets, which can provide for an abundant life today as well as tomorrow.

However, even with this holistic approach, our financial assets have inherent associated risks, and managing those risks must be a primary goal of integrated planning. Typical financial management strategies have done a poor job managing those risks as most cede control of your assets to financial and government institutions—severely limiting access and the ability to take advantage of new opportunities. Principal is most often at risk. This contributes to more uncertainty about your financial legacy. You just cannot count on what you want to have happen will happen.

Contrast this with an integrated approach where financial strategies focus on protecting family resources from market instabilities and other major risks while keeping them under the family's control. These are based on common-sense principles and strategies that preceded the rise of the financial and estate planning industries as we know them today. It's the family's nonfinancial asset strategies that drive consistent financial results.

This approach is important for all families, especially those still in the early stages of wealth-building. When all assets are capitalized, they form a foundation for building a strong, enduring legacy enriched by the family's economic, political, and social involvement.

THE FAMILY PROSPERITY SOLUTION™

We call our integrated planning approach the Family Prosperity Solution. No matter the level or complexity of the financial resources, it provides many of the following benefits. And these benefits rise in proportion to the family's commitment and participation in the process. Our solution:

- Unifies the family around shared principles, values, vision, and mission.
- Fosters a shared spirit of helping each other grow and follow individual pursuits.
- Enables family members to leverage the entirety of the family resources.
- Provides the family with sound financial education, and establishes a strong program of financial skills and habits successfully practiced by multiple generations.
- Creates good stewards of the family wealth with accountability and responsibility.
- Retains choice and control over the family wealth.
- Fuels a successful multigenerational legacy.

There is a continuum, from simple to sophisticated, for implementing this approach. Time and cost vary accordingly—yours and the advisor's. It requires a family leader, most often the wealth-creator, who will inspire family members to come together to get started and keep going. But this active family participation can be fun and rewarding. The results are far more powerful in identifying what you and your family want, and they'll provide a family prosperity blueprint to create and build wealth from generation to generation.

Let's look at how to get started.

Below is an overview of the three parts of the Family Prosperity

Solution. The parts are flexible, and they accomplish different, yet equally important, things:
- Prepare your family for your money.
- Prepare your money for your family.
- Protect and grow your money.

The first part is the most critical because it addresses the family's work with nonfinancial assets. The remaining two parts focus on implementation and integrating the money to power the family's aspirations and plans in the first part. They highlight some uncommon structures, strategies, and new responsibilities, which ensure that the financial resources will be there so that you and your family can achieve your goals and make your plans a reality.

Prepare Your Family for the Money

The processes and documents developed in this part address the unique work done together as a family.

Family assets, vision, and mission: The family together identifies and ranks their most important assets, starting with the nonfinancial ones. They create a family purpose, vision, and mission based on these ranked values. Methods to access this new family capital from a "family bank" are established.

Family philosophy: The wealth creator, along with the family, will write a family philosophy document. It describes your values, ethics, and aspirations for yourself and family members to ensure financial resources and strategies are in alignment. Some include religious beliefs, as well as positions on important social, political, and financial issues—whatever you feel is influential in driving the financial decisions you make and how you invest, grow, and use your wealth.

Family governance: The family creates guidelines that provide the structure for using and growing all assets. This includes the who, what, when, and how of depositing and withdrawing assets from the family bank. For example, a rule might outline when loans vs. gifts are made to family members and what the money can be used for. Using written rules, specific situations are addressed—such as how to help family members when there are extreme health issues or hardships, or when there are exceptional opportunities for investment, travel, or education. Some families with more complicated sets of assets create a board of directors composed of family members/professional advisors to manage these processes.

Communication and practice: Practice and exposure for family members is key as there are new concepts, and each family member needs to have a vested interest in the process. Regular meetings or planned family retreats provide critical time for the entire family to contribute. In addition to sharing experiences, it's a good opportunity to refine the family purpose or review family bank procedures and address other challenging questions.

Prepare Your Money for Your Family

In this part, the focus is on implementation: seeing that the right structures, rules, and relationships between family members and professional advisors exist to ensure your wealth (both financial and nonfinancial) is accessible, well-managed, and safeguarded. And most important, supports your family philosophy.

Family bank: The family bank is both a concept and a real repository for family assets. It can be simple or more complex, depending on the type of assets and the rules for accessibility and control. It plays a critical role as a resource to enable future generations to succeed by supporting their individual pursuits, including philanthropy. When each member has access to family resources, it fosters accountability, responsibility, and contribution. Regardless of the structure or complexity, it provides good money education and encourages hard work and discipline.

Advisory professionals and estate documents: Check to see if your current advisors (tax, legal, and financial) are knowledgeable about holistic planning and whether they want to work with a longer planning time frame than typical advisors. This is an ongoing, relationship-driven planning process, with a multigenerational vision for the family, so you want to make sure your advisor shares this long-term view. They should be willing to educate the family on the new requirements, structures, and legal and tax implications of managing the resources from the family bank. They should also know the family philosophy and ensure it provides the foundation for their planning and ongoing guidance. Implementation most often requires review and updating of your traditional estate documents, trusts, and other legal structures.

Protect and Grow Your Money

This part focuses on creating or amending financial plans so they are aligned with the family purpose and vision. Unique and uncommon money principles and strategies are there to support this long-term vision and keep it thriving and relevant for generations. It requires an open mind. At their core, these processes and strategies have the following principles:

Eliminate major risks for core financial assets. It's vital that a financial model is adopted that provides a safe money foundation for the family—one that provides 100 percent protection for your principal, achieves consistent returns without volatility, and protects against things you cannot control: major risks, such as financial and real estate market volatility; high taxation and inflation; catastrophic illness and job loss; liability; premature death and longevity; and the uncertainties of world events. This begins with drawing a clear distinction between savings (principal 100 percent protected) and investments (principal with associated levels of risk), and ensuring a good balance between the two.

Focus on cash flow, liquid reserves, and money leakages. Focus on cash flow, not net worth, to sustain lifestyle and achieve objectives. Choose and structure assets to retain control and maintain their liquidity to take advantage of opportunities or solve unexpected challenges. Systematically identify and minimize money leakages.

Educate the family on a sustainable financial model. As each successive generation builds on the financial knowledge and know-how, the family bank will evolve to remain relevant and to "fund" an expanding family vision/mission. Even with modest financial resources, simply educating the family by using the banking concept should soon result in the family asking for more in-depth financial education and needing a more sophisticated bank to support their growing wealth.

TWO ICONIC FAMILIES. TWO APPROACHES. TWO DIFFERENT RESULTS.

Born poor and with only a mediocre education, Cornelius Vanderbilt became one of the richest Americans in history, and per his instructions, his fortune was divided among his heirs. As noted in the book, The Fall of the House of Vanderbilt, by Arthur T. Vanderbilt, no one, except one son, increased their wealth. Within 30 years of Vanderbilt's death, no member of the Vanderbilt family was among the richest in the United States. And 48 years after his death, one of his grandchildren is said to have died penniless.

The Vanderbilts held a family reunion at Vanderbilt University in 1973, attended by 120 family members. Not one of them was even a millionaire. Not only had the family fortune been lost but also the knowledge that created that fortune. Arthur T. Vanderbilt reports that there was virtually no structure or organization in how the family transferred wealth from one generation to the next.

Contrast this with the Rothschild family: Soon after his sons became adults, the family patriarch, Mayer Rothschild, a first-generation banker, formed a wealth management structure with his five sons that codified how they would preserve and grow their wealth. Meeting routinely and coordinating family activities, the Rothschilds grew their businesses across Europe. Family members understood that the wealth was there as an enduring legacy.

Almost two centuries later, after multiple generational transfers of their wealth, the Rothschilds continue to be well-known and respected as a wealthy, philanthropic, and highly successful business family. Today, their global businesses have a value that far exceeds that first bank started by the family patriarch.

The Smiths. The Joneses. And the Rothschilds.

What the Rothschilds created was an early model for the family bank and a way of leveraging all their family assets. But this model is not the sole domain of the ultra-wealthy. It works for the Smiths and Joneses too.

Any family, no matter the size of their assets, can implement a modern-day version of family banking. All you need is family leadership and intent, and guidelines to set it up and get the family onboard. Whether we're talking about the Rothschilds or the Smiths and Joneses, it all comes down to the same factors.

Your leadership creates the family bank and governance framework. Your openness and willingness to share will engage the family. Your commitment will provide sound financial education, skills, and practices to your family. Your trust will empower the family to be good stewards of your legacy.

The impact and simplicity of this integrated approach can make a difference for you and your family right now, regardless of what stage you have achieved in your wealth building or estate planning.

An enduring legacy is all about what you instill when you are alive, not what you dictate after you're gone.

It's all about living an abundant life and creating living legacies that flourish from generation to generation. Start building your winning multigenerational family team today.

It's never too early or too late.

About the Author

Marilyn Johnson is the Founding Principal of Highgate Financial Advisors, a firm with a unique approach based on growing and managing both financial and nonfinancial assets. Highgate works with family members to leverage shared values, create common financial literacy, and instill collaborative practices across generations to make responsible wealth management choices. This approach, combined with sound financial strategies, produces true multi-generational prosperity solutions.

With experience as a Certified Financial Architect, mortgage planner, Infinite Banking Practitioner, and Circle of Wealth Certified Master Mentor, as well as her MBA in Finance from the Darden Business School at the University of Virginia, Marilyn's work supports a broad range of client needs.

Adventurous in spirit, she has lived and worked internationally, climbed Mt. Kilimanjaro, and mentored teenagers with refugee status to achieve their dream of a college education. Today, Marilyn lives a bi-coastal life with family, offices, and homes in California and Virginia.

Marilyn can be reached through HighGateCapitalGroup.com.

Jim Kindred

Chapter 4

What Your Banker Won't Tell You: Keys to the Bank for Small Business Owners

If you're like most entrepreneurs, you are always looking for ways to reduce costs and your income tax burden. You have a good CPA/accountant, but every tax season he recommends taking money from your current cash flow to fund a 401(k), SEP, or similar government-promoted retirement plan to reduce your taxes today to provide retirement income later. Reducing your taxes sounds great, but your business needs more cash flow, not less.

Instinctively, you know taking money out of your business today—and locking it up for 30 to 40 years (or more) in the Wall Street Casino to save taxes today, so you can potentially pay higher taxes in retirement—does not make economic sense. It violates the first two rules of business: Access to capital is critical, and cash is king.

Wouldn't it be nice to reduce your taxes today, provide a guaranteed tax-free retirement you can't outlive, and fund your business at the same time . . . with the same money?

For example, what if I gave you $100,000 to put into your business, with no stipulation as to how that money could be used? You could use the money in any way you saw fit. You could use it to finance your payroll, buy more equipment, hire more employees, provide more employee benefits, buy real estate, refinance equipment, create a new revenue stream, or expand your business.

What rate of return would YOU earn if that $100,000 were in YOUR business? I bet you could easily get 10 percent or more... think of your margins. How does that compare with the returns your financial advisor or accountant is saying you might get by locking up your money?

What if you could put any amount of money into an account that would allow you to create wealth for your retirement, while at the same time allowing you to use that money for any investment or lending strategy you could conceive? What if you could invest in or lend money to your business, your wife, or your children for college—or use it for down payments on their first home, starting or expanding a business, or whatever you think makes a good investment?

And what if that money were growing state and federal income tax free? And you could access whatever wealth you created in this account at retirement, income tax and penalty free, while at the same time providing a tax-free death benefit to your family or your business in the event of your premature death?

You're in Luck!

Fortunately, there is such an account that does all of the above and also addresses the inflation and longevity issues older Americans are so keenly aware of, while reducing your taxes now and in retirement—and it does so without requiring government approval or involvement.

You won't find this account promoted by your investment advisor or CPA as a "retirement plan," nor will you find it listed among the 401(k), 403(b), 457, or other popular qualified plans or formal retirement schemes.

Why? Because it is not a plan or a qualified plan. So, you will not be fettered by the restrictions of age, contribution limits, how your money can be used, early or late withdrawal fees, etc. Conversely, conventional retirement plans are regulated by the Department of Labor, which dictates all of the above, and then some.

Section 7702 of the Internal Revenue Code describes private contracts between individuals with mutual goals and aspirations. This section is where the tax benefits and requirements of life insurance are enumerated. These plans are ideally suited to small business owners who understand the best place to invest is in their own businesses. Although permanent life insurance has been around for over 200 years, it remains largely misunderstood and underused.

The Ideal Financial Vehicle

If you could create the ideal financial vehicle, what would it look like? Consider these basic benefits:

You could put away any amount you could afford—far more money for retirement than your Keogh, SEP, 401(k), or other government plans will allow.

The money in the account earns a guaranteed, reasonable, competitive, fixed rate of return on a foundation of multiple guarantees, without being at risk in the stock market.

You could outperform all government-sponsored retirement plans.

The funds in the account could be protected from creditors (depending on your state).

The account has the ability to earn tax-free dividends while you are growing your business, then when you are ready to retire, the full account can be accessed income tax free, and/or used to leverage other nonperforming assets.

The cash in the account can be accessed at any time, for any reason. You can manage the money or let the insurance company do it for you, which means you could use the money now (in your business) and in retirement—without limitation, fees, or penalties. You control everything! So, with proper planning and design, you could create additional ways to increase the tax advantages and benefits of your business, such as converting your liabilities into assets (the way your banker does) and converting earned income into investment income, thus lowering your self-employment tax.

You can guarantee and ensure that what you want to have in retirement will be there, regardless of your health or ability to continue working, and what money you don't use in your later years can be transferred to your heirs without probate, income, or estate tax.

By coordinating with your other assets, including the disposition of your business at retirement, you could either increase your overall retirement income by 30 to 150 percent or more, or gain 30 to 50 percent more free time now.

You can create your own private, personal financing system to gradually replace your personal and business bankers, putting you in charge of what your banker previously controlled. (How great would that be?)

While government-promoted retirement plans do only one thing—provide money for retirement—you can now have one dollar doing the work of several. How many tasks each dollar performs will be up to you and your creativity. An experienced financial strategist can be invaluable in finding ways to optimize your benefits.

I know this sounds too good to be true. It did to me, too, the first time I heard about it. But so did cell phones, television, airplanes, the Internet, and Jell-O the first time I was introduced to them.

In a Class by Itself

Permanent life insurance, optimized with high cash values, is an asset class all by itself. All other asset classes—including mutual funds, stocks, bonds, ETFs, real estate, gold, etc.—are what I like to call "OR" assets. You either have your money in one asset class or another, but not both. In other words, you couldn't have the same dollars in two places at once (e.g. invested in a mutual fund while also invested in your business).

However, permanent life insurance is what I like to call an "AND" asset. It's the only one of its kind that enables you to keep your money in two places at once. So, how can you benefit from owning this type of asset?

Assume for a moment you have $100,000 in a liquid account, such as a business checking account, money market, or simply in savings. Why do you hold money in these kinds of accounts? Simple. You inherently understand that access to capital trumps potential rates of return in risky investment accounts where market volatility adds unnecessary risk. Likewise, money tied up in markets, such as real estate, is not liquid. As you well know, investments can turn out to be great, not so great, or even disappear altogether. This means investment accounts are not suitable places to hold the money critical to your business.

Because you have been living in an "OR" asset world, you've probably never heard of "AND" assets (and, therefore, do not know how they work). So, let's look at an example and assume you want to purchase some equipment for your business.

There are three ways to make major purchases, two of which you are intimately familiar; the third will be new to you. Which strategy is best?

1. The saver's strategy (paying cash)
2. The borrower's strategy (using other people's money—OPM)
3. The Replace Your Banker strategy (a collateralized way of using OPM)

Historically, you had two choices for making major purchases: You could either pay cash, or you could finance it. (Obviously, you could enter into a lease, but, in the final analysis, a lease is still a borrowing strategy, with some perceived tax advantages.)

When you pay cash, the money you had in a checking or savings account will be spent—the money is gone, never to be seen again. But it's actually worse than that. When you pay cash, not only is the cash gone, but you also gave away the opportunity for that cash to earn for you ever again.

Your second choice is to leave your cash alone and borrow the money you need. But in this strategy, you lose not only the cost of what you were buying (the principal), but also the interest. And with this strategy, you will have structured payments. Should you be late or miss a payment, your banker will report you to the credit bureaus, creating increased borrowing costs in the future.

If you look closely at both scenarios, you gave up the principal and the interest in each strategy. You either passed up the interest you would have earned had you left the money in the account (where it would've been working for you), or you gave up interest to the banker to borrow his money.

Let's look at a third, outside-the-box strategy.

What if you owned the bank? What if you could borrow the principal from your own private bank at a rate you got to choose—plus you could set all the rest of the terms, including the payment schedule, fees, penalties, etc.—just like your corner banker does? Here is the important question: If you were the lender, at the end of the loan repayment period, where would the principal and interest be? (Take the time to ponder this.)

That's right, the principal you spent and the interest you paid would be back in your bank, instead of your corner banker's bank! And that money would be ready for your next deal.

The Replace Your Banker Strategy (The Best of Both Worlds)

Remember that "AND" account we spoke about earlier? Because the money inside the whole life policy is accessible, you could now become the preferred lender for your business. Simply by changing the way you "finance" the major purchases you plan to make anyway, you can increase your wealth by financing your business. Are you beginning to see what your corner banker sees?

One of the major purposes of your corner banker is to turn liabilities into assets. They convert your liabilities into their assets!

Do you know anyone who has liabilities? In their business, personal, or family life? Everyone has liabilities. Today, in your current situation, who benefits from your liabilities? I bet it's not you! And if it's not you, what difference does it make who benefits?

In the Replace Your Banker Strategy, we make contributions into an account the same way as in the saver's example—except we put those dollars into a whole life policy. Where we deposit those funds and how we use them once they are deposited can make a huge difference. Like the saver's strategy, we have an initial "capitalization period" as we fund our permanent, dividend-paying, whole life insurance contract. Whole life insurance is built on a foundation of multiple guarantees, none of which are tied to the investment risks of the stock market. That means when you want access to capital, you know the money will be there, for your use. The mutual insurance company will hold your funds and lend you the money for any purpose—business or pleasure.

Consider this: When you take a home equity line of credit, you pledge your home's value to borrow the bank's money. You are not borrowing YOUR money. Instead, you are pledging your real property as collateral to borrow the bank's money. Let me repeat: It is not your money you are borrowing! Taking a loan against a life insurance policy works the exact same way—with one huge, notable exception. Whether you take a loan or let the account grow, the underlying policy values continue to increase at a guaranteed rate (something you wish your home and other assets could do). The compound growth curve is, therefore, unaffected and continues to increase at a predetermined, guaranteed internal growth rate. By pledging your policy as collateral to the insurance company, you borrow the insurance company's money rather than yours.

Are there tax advantages to borrowing from an insurance company, then lending that money to your business? When your business pays back a loan, can it deduct that interest expense? Would this give you another way to take money out of your business . . . on a favorable tax basis? Are there strategies where you could begin re-characterizing some of your ordinary income as investment income? Would that lower your taxes this year? Could some of the things you have been paying cash for now be financed . . . using an account you control? Think of the possibilities—they are almost endless!

Just the Beginning

There are many ways dividend-paying whole life insurance can benefit your business. While the cash values can be used pay off debts and liabilities, the results are even better when used to finance income-producing assets, such as real estate, operational capital, and capital expenditures of every kind. You are limited only by your imagination, which can enhance revenue streams now and create tax-advantaged income streams in retirement.

Remember we finance everything we buy. We either pass up interest by borrowing money or pass up interest by using our own cash.

If you have a successful business, you have all the tools to begin replacing your banker. All you need are the keys to the bank to help you capitalize on what your corner banker has been doing since the inception of your business: turning liabilities into assets. Once you begin to think like a banker, you will begin to see financing opportunities within your business you didn't know existed.

One final word: permanent whole life insurance has some great tax advantages. Because these accounts are private, they afford coordination of benefit opportunities that go far beyond what has been introduced here. According to nationally syndicated CPA and tax expert Ed Slott, "The single biggest benefit in the federal tax code is provided by permanent life insurance," which "should be the bedrock of any serious financial, retirement, or estate plan." He also thinks these policies are "not used nearly enough."

I could not agree more.

About the Author

As a small business owner, former senior management, and human resources consultant, Jim Kindred's real-life experience as a "loaned executive" in economic development uniquely qualifies him to provide valuable financial strategies for successful entrepreneurs.

Few business owners know how to benefit from the money that flows continuously through their businesses. Instead, they unknowingly and unnecessarily give away wealth that could otherwise be theirs... if they were to learn the keys to the bank. Once they understand the keys their bankers use to keep them beholding to them, these entrepreneurs secure control over their businesses they did not know was possible.

Jim can be reached at Jim@InfoWest.com.

Anthony J. Faso, CPA

Chapter 5

I Kid You Not:
Why You Should Place a Life Insurance Policy on Your Child

I've been asked many times, "Why would anyone place a life insurance policy on their child?" However, there are many reasons a parent or grandparent should consider this.

When someone thinks about life insurance, they are typically thinking about a death benefit. That can be important, even on a child, but it should not be the sole reason for life insurance on a child. In addition to a death benefit, life insurance can also provide cash value. When structured correctly, the cash value can grow and be accessible tax free. In this chapter, we'll be discussing how the death benefit and cash value from a life insurance policy can be used to create a financial safety net for the family.

Life Insurance Defined

Before we begin, let's define what we mean by "life insurance." There are many types of life insurance. Most of you are familiar with term insurance, which builds no cash value and, in essence, is renting a death benefit for a specific period of time. Over the last 30 to 40 years, new types of life insurance have been created. You may have heard of variable universal life, index universal life, or universal life. These new types of life insurance provide a death benefit and the possibility of cash value. I say "possibility" because the performance of many of these policies is tied to the stock market. So, in times of low performance or a financial crisis, the policy can go bankrupt.

Throughout this book, when we refer to life insurance, we are talking about whole life insurance. Whole life insurance has been around for over 200 years, and the performance of whole life policies is not tied to the stock market. As for insurance companies, we recommend using a mutual insurance company. Mutual insurance companies are not owned by stockholders or traded on Wall Street; they are owned by policyholders. The profits generated by a mutual insurance company are paid as dividends to its owners. However, instead of going to stockholders, these profits go to the policyholders. In other words, you and me.

On a side note, dividends from a stock company are taxable, similar to dividends from other stocks, like Bank of America or General Electric. However, dividends from a mutual life insurance company are tax free. In addition, there are numerous mutual life insurance companies that have been around for over 150 years—and have paid a dividend each one of those years. That means they paid a dividend during the Great Recession and the Great Depression.

Death Benefit

When I first talk to a parent about life insurance on their child, their initial reaction is that the last thing they want to do, if they lost a child, would be to profit from their loss. I agree wholeheartedly. My question is, "Do you want to compound an emotional loss with a financial loss?"

Some may question whether financial loss exits with the loss of the child. For example, most parents do not rely on their children to help pay the bills. However, when a family loses a child, there are typically a large number of medical bills and expenses to lay the child to rest.

Many concerns and questions arise when enduring a catastrophic loss. Here are a few:

If you lost a child, would you go to work the next day? What about the next week? The next month?

When you went back to work, do you think you'd be at your best? Typically, it takes a few years for a parent's productivity to get back to the way it was.

If you took a couple months off work, would you have trouble paying your bills?

Would you need grief counseling?

Would you want to live in the same house? Would you want to move?

What if housing prices were down, and you were under water and couldn't sell your home for more than what you owe?

Do you think the loss of a child would affect your marriage? I've been told that 50 percent of marriages fail after the loss of a child. How would that impact your other children or your finances?

Illness

Under certain conditions, many insurance companies allow policy owners to receive an advance of the death benefit while the insured person is still alive. These funds can be used when the insured has a critical illness or is terminally ill. There are typically no restrictions on how you spend the money. You can use these benefits as you choose.

The son of a dear friend of mine graduated college and was about to fulfill his dream of joining the Coast Guard. All the paperwork was complete; he knew where he was going to be stationed and what his job was going to be. All he had to do was pass the physical. He was only 22, and if you asked him, he was healthy as a horse. But the physical revealed he had a lump on his testicle. It turned out that he had testicular cancer. They also found masses on his stomach and brain. The doctors gave him a 50-50 chance to survive.

Unfortunately, his health insurance did not cover all his medical expenses. Very few, in fact. If his parents wanted their oldest son to survive, they were going to have to pay out of pocket. Faced with that choice, who wouldn't sell everything they had to provide their child with the best chance of survival?

If they would have had a life insurance policy on their son, they would have been able to use a portion of the death benefit, while he was alive, to pay the medical expenses. This would not only ensure he had the best care, but the stress of finding the money to pay for the expenses could have been minimal or even avoided. His family could have focused on physical healing, rather than worry about financial healing.

College Planning

Most parents believe the only smart way to set aside money for college is a 529 Plan—but life insurance can be an ideal savings vehicle for this purpose. In fact, it was not all that long ago, in 1996, when Congress started allowing 529 Plans to be used as a college investing tool.

A 529 Plan allows parents or grandparents to set aside money for their child or grandchild to be used for college. If the money is used directly for college, all the withdrawals will be tax free. But what happens if they don't use the money for college? We will address that in a few paragraphs.

Notice I called a 529 Plan a college "investing" tool, not a college "savings" tool. There's a big difference between savings and investing. I define savings as money I cannot afford to lose and investing as money that I can. I hate to lose money, which is why I am very careful when I invest.

I lost money with my son's 529 plan. He made the "mistake" of being a junior in high school during the 2008 crash. He lost 60 percent of the college money inside his 529 Plan. He was going to college in two years, and we lost more than half of what we had set aside. That doesn't sound like a great college "savings" plan to me.

Since many families use a 529 Plan for their college fund, it's important to know how colleges view 529 Plans when they're calculating how much financial aid to give to a family. There are two different calculations schools use to calculate your financial aid. There is the Free Application for Federal Student Aid, commonly referred to as the FAFSA; this is what most colleges use. Ivy leagues and some private schools use the CSS Profile. The FAFSA counts the value of a 529 Plan the same as any asset of the parents. The more money you have in a 529 Plan or investment account, the less financial aid you will receive.

A CSS Profile school can account for the 529 plan however they want to. They can count it as an asset of the parent or of the child, or they can count it as income of the parent or of the child.

Imagine you're the financial aid officer for the school and you see two applications. One student has $100,000 in the 529 Plan and the other student has zero. Are you going to give more financial aid to the student who doesn't have a 529 Plan? Thus, more money will be given to the family that prepared the least.

So, where does life insurance fit into all this? Well, the cash value of life insurance is not counted on the FAFSA. A CSS Profile may count some of the cash value in your life insurance, however, they are more likely to count the money inside a 529 Plan.

What happens if your child doesn't go to college? Our society pushes our children to go to college, but college is not for everyone. What if your child wants to learn a trade or start a business? Also, what happens if your student has more money in their 529 Plan than the costs for them to go to college? Any gain inside the 529 Plan will be taxable at your ordinary tax rate, plus a 10 percent penalty. The gain is the difference between your contributions and the current balance. If your contributions into the 529 Plan total $80,000 and the current balance is $100,000, your gain would be $20,000. Let's say you're in the 30 percent tax bracket (25 percent for federal income tax and let's not forget your lovely 5 percent state income tax). That means a 10 percent penalty would be $8,000 (30% + 10% = 40% of $20,000).

So, how can you use the cash value of life insurance to pay for college expenses? Well, you can take a loan against your cash value and use the proceeds for anything you deem necessary, including college expenses, a trade school, or to start a new business. It would not be fair to make a broad statement and suggest that you should not have any money inside the 529 Plan. However, it is fair to say that you should know all your options, as well as the potential risks and tax consequences. With the limits and tax consequences of a 529 Plan, why would you not have some of your college funding inside the cash value of a life insurance policy?

Family Banking

Nelson Nash is the author of the book *Becoming Your Own Banker* and the creator of the Infinite Banking Concept. In his book, Nelson describes how you can use the cash value of a whole life policy to create your own banking system. In simple terms, instead of borrowing money from a bank and paying interest, you borrow from your whole life policy. Instead of paying the bank interest, you pay the interest to your policy. My discussion here does not do justice to explaining the Infinite Banking Concept, so I highly encourage you to read Nelson's book.

My wife and I want to encourage our children to not have to rely on commercial banks for their financing needs. We are educating them to rely on the family bank (i.e., the cash value of their life insurance policy). The best way we can encourage them is to create and use their own family bank for their major purchases. For example, they can finance their first car, college education, a business, or even the latest and greatest game console. It doesn't matter what it is or how much it is—what is important is that they learn to borrow and repay themselves as opposed to somebody else.

Legacy

What is a legacy? The Merriam-Webster dictionary defines legacy as:
Something (such as property or money) that is received from someone who has died;
Something that happened in the past or that comes from someone in the past.

Many times we focus on the property and money part. We think of legacy as leaving money to our family and favorite charities. I think legacy is much bigger than that. I like to say that legacy is not only dollars, but it is also sense. If we leave our kids a pile of money without the wisdom to handle it, we could be doing them more harm than good.

So, where does life insurance factor into all of this? Well, it can be used to pass down money, and if used correctly, to pass on wisdom. When the child is a minor, the parent or grandparent (or whoever is paying the premium) should be the owner. Upon the death of the owner, the ownership of the life insurance policy can pass to the child. Hopefully, by this time, the child is an adult; if not, the ownership should go into a trust.

My wife and I are using our kid's life insurance policies to fund their higher-education expenses. Each year or semester when the tuition is due, we take a policy loan to pay for the expenses. Upon graduation, we will present our child with a graduation gift. Part of that gift will be the loan against the life insurance policy. It may sound odd to give a loan to someone as a present. We are going to tell them that, in the workforce, most of their co-workers are going to have student loans. They should treat their policy loans as student loans and pay them back. Their co-workers are contributing to their IRAs or 401(k)s. Our kids should instead start paying the premiums on their polices.

If they do not pay back the loans or start paying the premiums, I am still the owner of the policy, which means I wouldn't need to give them the policy now—or ever. Why would I? If they are not going to be a good money steward when they are making a little, how are they going to do so when they're making a lot or if/when they receive their inheritance? At that point, we have a few options:

We could sell the policy. (This would be my last resort, but it is an option.)

We could cash in the policy and get all the cash value back minus any loans we took out.

We could tell the insurance company we don't want to make premiums anymore, and they can mark the policy "paid up." This means the death benefit is recalculated based on fewer premiums being paid; however, the cash value will be the same and it will continue to grow.

We could keep the policies along with the cash value for ourselves and continue to educate our children until they prove they can handle this gift.

If they prove to be good money stewards, we will gift them their policies. Their savings will be in a safe vehicle; in fact, in one of the safest available. Hopefully, they will do the same for their children, and this becomes a family tradition. We will feel comfortable that we left them a legacy not just in dollars but also in sense.

No Question About It

We started this chapter with the question: "Why would anyone ever place a life insurance policy on a child?" After knowing all that life insurance can do, I think a better question is: "Why would anyone not place a life insurance policy on their child?"

About the Author

Anthony J. Faso is a self-described "Recovering CPA." After working for the accounting firm PricewaterhouseCoopers and owning his own CPA firm, Anthony now focuses his practice on teaching Prosperity Economics to families and business owners. His goal is to enable them to "build wealth beyond Wall Street" without trying to rely on the roller-coaster returns of conventional investing.

Anthony lives in Las Vegas, Nevada with his wife and two kids. He also served in the US Army and is an avid Pittsburgh Steelers fan. To learn more about Anthony, check out AnthonyFaso.com or @FasoCPA on Twitter.

Gina C. Wells

Chapter 6

A Balancing Act: Using Leverage to Build Your Financial Nest Egg

Balancing is hard work. Positive and negative forces influence your decisions about money, continually forcing you to teeter back and forth. It takes effort and power to return to the positive side. The longer you languish in the center, the more time, effort, and energy you'll spend trying to stay there. Holding on to what you have, without fighting the odds, simply waiting for the next problem to occur, hinders your opportunity to gain the required momentum needed to get and stay on the top.

How the US Treasury Leverages Tax Dollars—and Its Effect on Your Retirement

Our federal government leverages how they collect and spend tax dollars based on many factors. The balancing act includes weighing current taxation against future taxation. One area that is documented annually is the amount of "pre-tax" money in retirement programs such as IRAs and 401(k)s.

In retirement, your taxable income is generated from your investment accounts, pensions, and social security payments. In 1993, the Omnibus Budget Reconciliation Act raised the proportion of social security benefits that can be taxed as income—from 50 percent to 85 percent—on retirees who reach specific income thresholds. This, of course, created a greater tax burden on qualifying retirees. What they had expected to be reduced taxation in retirement turned out to be the opposite—effectively counter-balancing their future income plans.

All financial institutions are required to report to the IRS the year-end balances of all "pre-tax" accounts (i.e., accounts made up of money that has not yet been taxed). IRS form 5498 is mailed out in January for individual IRAs; form 5500 is filed in December for pre-tax dollars held in employer-sponsored plans. These reporting documents serve two purposes:

They are used to leverage future tax revenue—in other words, the federal government makes spending decisions and borrows against this money it will collect in the future.

They alert the US Treasury to individuals who have reached age 70½ and are now forced to take a distribution percentage from all of their combined pre-tax accounts—known as the "Required Minimum Distribution" or "RMD" for short.

If a retiree does not take this RMD, they will suffer a 50-percent penalty on the amount they did not withdraw during the applicable tax year. However, the IRS generally will not find these discrepancies until years later and will notify the retiree by a letter that basically states:

Mr. Retiree,

Your 5498 forms for the calendar year 2017 totaled $200,000 and you withdrew $2,000. Your Required Minimum Distribution was $7,547.17. A 50 percent penalty plus tax is being imposed on the difference of $5,547.17. You owe an additional $1,109 in federal income tax, plus the penalty of $2,774.

The longer you delay paying the additional amount, the greater the interest will be charged, and you will owe even more.
Sincerely,
The Internal Revenue Service

So, as you plan for retirement, be sure you understand that you are postponing paying tax at today's rate when you deposit your income into a pre-tax retirement account. It would be great to know that you had postponed paying, for example, a 20-percent rate today on wages and ultimately accessed those same dollars in a lower tax bracket in retirement—leverage would be on your side! However, the odds are against being in a lower tax bracket in years to come. Due to inflation, the same standard of living in retirement as you have today will require you to be in the same or a higher tax bracket. Hoping to be in a lower tax bracket is basically hoping to be worse off in retirement!

The question you should be asking today is, "Can my current pre-tax contributions be effectively leveraged against future taxation?" If you can honestly forecast that the tax-deferred money you're contributing now will earn enough to sustain your lifestyle in retirement—and you'll have enough left over to pay the deferred tax that will be due—then read no further. However, if you are beginning to understand that these pre-tax accounts held by financial institutions are not in your best interest (as they're subject to investment risk and give you no early access to your money without incurring penalties and taxes), then now is the time to find and develop a "counter-balance."

Who Ultimately Benefits from Leveraged Taxation?

President George W. Bush signed the Worker, Retiree, and Employer Recovery Act of 2008, essentially giving tax-paying retirees over the age of 70½ a one-year reprieve from having to take RMDs.

Did the President and Congress really do those individuals a favor, or did this benefit the government? As you will see, it depends on where a retiree was teetering on the fulcrum.

Ultimately, the goal of that legislation was to help the government stay balanced on the fulcrum. The reality for retirees, however, was that it created leverage for some and took it away from others.

As you can see in Figure 6.1, the stock market saw a gain in 2009. That one-year gain was not enough to make up for the losses of the past year, but if time was on your side, then you could maintain stability. If the one-time reprieve did not matter to you because you had to withdraw the money to live on, then time was not on your side; you needed that withdrawal to survive. For those individuals, they did not fare as well—they lost leverage.

The next year, the market was up again, but still not enough to make up for the losses. What if you were dependent on that money sitting in your IRA and needed to take a distribution? Then you lost a tremendous amount of power having to sell assets in a down market.

Figure 6.1 shows the average rate of return (ROR) for years 2007 through 2014. The top row shows the overall average ROR for the entire eight-year period in each of the listed markets. (NOTE: The sequence of annual returns is very important when you are at-

AVERAGE ROR:	5.84%	6.96%	9.21%
Year	Dow Jones Industrials Without Dividends	S&P 500 Without Dividends	S&P 500 With Dividends
2007	4.56	3.53	5.51
2008	(30.74)	(38.49)	(36.83)
2009	17.15	23.45	25.85
2010	10.27	12.78	14.89
2011	6.23	(0.00)	2.23
2012	8.19	13.41	16.00
2013	22.58	29.60	32.23
2014	8.46	11.39	13.63

Figure 6.1

tempting to leverage your future retirement income. A major loss, as in 2008 in the chart, requires more than the equal percentage in later gains to get back to even. For example, if you have an investment valued at $100 that loses 30 percent, that investment is now valued at $70. But a subsequent gain of 30 percent (30 percent of $70) is $21, bringing you up to a value of only $91. To get back to $100 from $70 actually requires a gain of 43 percent.)

An account with $100,000 of pre-tax money would have experienced the past performance of the "S&P 500 With Dividends" as outlined in Figure 6.1. Now, let's use that performance as the basis for Figure 6.2.

In Figure 6.2, we calculate as if the "reprieve" was never given. It includes the assumption that the earnings from year one added to the beginning balance of $100,000 totals a 2007 year-end value of $105,510. This is the value that would have determined the RMD for 2008, which is listed as a withdrawal of $3,966 (at age 72) and

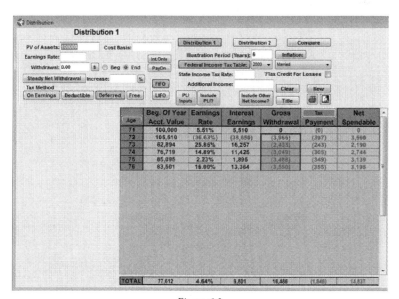

Figure 6.2

changes each year thereafter according to the beginning-year value. Now, Figure 6.3 assumes no withdrawal—the 2008 government reprieve. Comparing Figure 6.2 (as if no reprieve was given and the distribution was taken) to Figure 6.3 (no withdrawal was taken due to the reprieve), you can see that the government collected fewer tax dollars from our theoretical retiree in 2008 (see "Tax Payment" for "Age 72"). However, after the sixth year ("Age 76" in the chart), the tax on distributions begins to increase. The government was well aware of the balancing act needed in 2008 so as to not affect future taxation on pre-tax retirement accounts:

	Figure 6.2	Figure 6.3	Difference
Total Taxes Paid	$1,649	$1,301	$348 fewer tax dollars
7th-Year Beginning Value	$77,612	$82,287	$11,382 more IRA dollars
6th-Year Distribution	$3,550	$3,688	$138 more tax dollars AND GROWING…

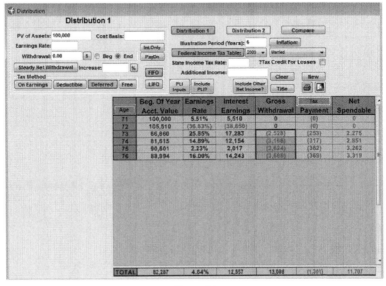

Figure 6.3

The methodology was to allow the IRA account values to recoup from the market loss of 2008, preserving future taxation on the accounts. Essentially, the government postponed collecting $348 in 2008 so that they would collect a greater amount of tax on an increasing account value in the years to come.

So who was it that lost the greatest balance on the fulcrum in 2008?

Figure 6.4 assumes a retiree taking a $5,000-per-year withdrawal, paying a flat tax of $500 per year over a five-year period, ending up with $69,521.

For the retiree outlined in Figure 6.4, had they stayed in the market, their overall loss during this time would have been 1.33 percent—in other words, they did not recover during this timeframe. (Figure 6.5 on the next page shows how that rate was determined. Starting with $100,000 in 2007, withdrawing $5,000 per year for five years, and ending up with a value of $69,521 is a return of negative 1.33 percent.)

Many retirees went back to work instead of continuing to with-

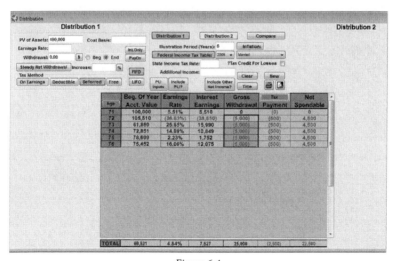

Figure 6.4

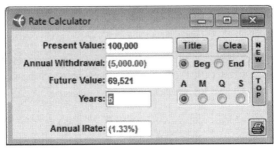

Figure 6.5

draw from their retirement accounts. Many liquidated their stock portfolios altogether for fear of another market crash. Many reduced their standard of living by finding ways to live on less. Others were able to use other assets as leverage in the market downturn, which helped them to stay on the positive side of the fulcrum.

Don't Wait to Build Positive Leverage

We have been talking about full retirees in the previous examples. For those of you who are still working and earning a paycheck, you have a chance to build the foundation of the fulcrum on which you balance your financial life. To stay on the positive side of leverage, you will need to protect your ability to not only earn a paycheck, but also to cash it, save it, and spend it. The longer you wait to build your leverage, the less you will have.

Your paycheck can be leveraged against many things:

Your ability to earn a paycheck: If you do not have your income protected against an accident or illness with disability insurance, you lose leverage. If you lose your job, you lose your leverage. At the time of retirement, if you have not saved enough to last until your death, you will lose leverage.

Your ability to cash your paycheck: If you cannot save money first and then pay your bills, you will lose leverage. Without a good credit score, the banking institutions will charge you more to access credit. You could also lose leverage in the event of a lawsuit, which may take a portion of your paycheck to pay back the judgment. Staying ahead of lawsuits, with proper property and casualty insurance for your home and auto, in addition to an umbrella policy, which covers liability over and above base auto and home coverages, will help you avoid unexpected losses.

Your ability to spend your paycheck: The ability to maintain the lifestyle you are currently living, adjusted for inflation over time, is dependent on the moves you make during your working years. Avoiding the losses along the way is more important that chasing rates of return. The goal in retirement is to spend and enjoy your money for your remaining lifetime and leave a legacy for your family or favorite charities.

Don't Procrastinate!

Waiting too long to address these issues is usually due to simple procrastination. But continuing on this path only costs you more time, money, and productivity. Understand that—for each dollar lost—you have lost both that dollar and what that dollar could have earned (through saving or investing) had you not lost it. This factor alone can become one of the heaviest burdens on your future benefits. If you can stop the money that is unknowingly and unnecessarily leaving your account, you will gain positive leverage for the future. Leverage is everything: The more you have, the better off you will be; the less you have, the more time, money, or energy you will need to harness in the future.

How to Reverse Opportunity Cost

In the paragraph above, the lost dollar is a cost; the inability to earn from that lost dollar is an example of opportunity cost. Think about the amount of money you will make from now until you retire. If you are making $100,000 a year for the next 20 years, two million dollars will move through your hands over that time period. Where will it all go?

Our main categories are taxes, debt, and lifestyle—under which you have specific categories like clothes, vacations, fees, college, rent, and so on. Then, you have costs related to your auto, home, liability, medical, and disability insurance coverage, which all essentially protect your lifestyle. Most of our lifestyle expenses (including insurance) are impacted by inflation—the increasing cost of the goods and services we use over our lifetime. For the purposes of this discussion, let's assume you are paying 20 percent in taxes, using 30 percent of your income to pay your debt, and spending 40 percent on yourself and family. That leaves 10 percent to divide into 5 percent for insurance protection and 5 percent for savings.

In this scenario, you will have put aside $5,000 per year for 20 years, totaling $100,000 in your savings account as contributions (i.e., not including interest earned). More is better, but how much is enough? What risks will you face? How can you leverage cost over benefit to gain greater momentum?

Take Charge of Your Future

Learning to change your cash flow and eliminate losses will allow you to gain greater benefits. For example, "debt restructuring" (reducing your debt obligation) will allow you to start saving the difference. In our scenario above, just reducing the debt portion of the spending from 30 to 25 percent would give you the ability to double your savings—to $200,000 at the end of year 20—without assuming additional risk or changing your lifestyle.

Every year that you procrastinate and avoid addressing the issues discussed above is another year you must double up on your savings or triple down on your spending. There is no time like the present to take charge of your situation. If you continue to procrastinate for another five years, you will have greatly diminished the amount of money in your control for future use and enjoyment.

Your Homework

Once you understand where your cash flow is going, do not wait. You need to understand what benefits you are generating from your hard-earned dollars—not only for today, but especially for the future. (For more on this, check out my blog post "Do You Have A Backup Plan?" at www.Advanced-CapitalGroup.com.)

Take an inventory of your assets and liabilities and what you spend your money on. If you can find any money that is unnecessarily moving away from you, plug the hole so your savings can begin to grow today. This alone will put you in a better position to leverage against future risks—increased taxation; inflation; spending on items like cars, college, or vacations; interest costs; health-care costs; job loss; disability; and ultimately, your legacy plan.

Leverage is an important term to add to your financial vocabulary. Use it daily. Learn to measure its benefits today and how those benefits will increase your future success.

About the Author

Gina C. Wells, CLU, ChFC has enjoyed a career which focuses on helping people build and keep wealth. Since 1994, she has dedicated herself to sharing with her clients her knowledge and experience of how money works on a personal level. By offering them consistency, integrity, and genuine concern, she has earned a reputation as a trustworthy advisor and friend. Gina is a member of the Infinite Banking Institute, a Prosperity Economics Advisor, and a Qualifying and Life Member of the Million-Dollar Round Table.

Gina can be reached through Advanced-CapitalGroup.com.

 John Householder

Chapter 7
Make No Mistake: How to Pay for College Without Breaking the Family Bank

Does thinking about college costs scare you? You aren't alone. In 20 years of college advising, I have met few families or students who are fully informed of their options. While I can't cover every aspect of college preparation here, I can steer you away from making some of the worst mistakes.

Mistake #1: You assume college is the only way your new high school graduate will be successful.

I know what the data says: A college graduate will make millions more over a lifetime than a non-grad, and the best investment you can make is in yourself. More and more career pathways also require a college education. I wholeheartedly believe in education and would never talk a student out of going to college and chasing their dreams. But that decision should be made knowing the real costs, including opportunity cost.

Let's consider a parent saving from age 35 to 45 to pay for her child's college tuition, putting aside $11,952 per year. Earning 6 percent interest, her savings would grow to $164,445 during that time—a healthy amount to cover typical state-college tuition and expenses for four years. (Our parent smartly factored in inflation when determining what to put aside each year, knowing tuition would likely be much higher by the time her child entered college.) But we still need to consider the opportunity cost.

Had our parent not paid the tuition, but kept that $164,445 invested at the same 6 percent growth rate until retirement at age 65, it would have accumulated to $608,810. Those dollars would have provided $41,670 per year in retirement income from age 65 to 90 (on top of social security or any other income). This is opportunity cost—opportunities given up as the result of a choice. Worse yet, if the student took six years to graduate instead of four, the opportunity cost rises to $913,215 with $62,505 in lost annual income from age 65 to 90. Does this get your attention?

Now consider 40 percent of college students do not make it through their bachelor's degrees, even after six years. Too many of those who do graduate within that six-year time frame finish with a different degree, chosen only because it was an easier path to graduation. All too often, the new major has much bleaker job prospects.

Perhaps it's time to give more thought to if and when our students are ready for college. Even top high school graduates with many academic scholarship offers on the table should consider timing. Taking a year to travel or do something spectacular in a field of interest makes a strong resume even better, and it also provides experience and builds maturity prior to starting college. Conversely, placing a student in college before they have demonstrated the maturity, social skills, self-discipline, or desire to succeed is a recipe not just for failure, but it may also have lifelong unintended consequences.

There are also many students who would be much better off apprenticing or starting their own business. Quite a few companies pay for their employee's college coursework as a way to keep their best and provide a path to corporate positions. The armed services and some nonprofits like the Peace Corp also give fantastic college benefit packages to those who are willing to serve first before going to college. Seeking and selecting the right time and path may be more important than searching for higher savings or lower costs.

Mistake #2: You think all higher-cost schools are unaffordable

When considering colleges, there are three major components in the net out-of-pocket costs: the sticker price of the college, scholarships and grants offered, and expected family contribution (EFC). Unless you attend a very low-cost college, your EFC is the minimum you can expect to pay to go to any university. The EFC is unique to each family and results from what you submit to the government on the Free Application of Federal Student Aid (FAFSA). Your FAFSA input is based on your assets and income as of January in your student's senior year. Some colleges also use the CSS Profile in lieu of, or in addition to, the FAFSA, but it meets the same purpose. For now, just understand the FAFSA and CSS Profile determine your EFC, and, as colleges term it, your "financial need." Colleges are not required to meet your full financial need, but for comparison purposes, let's see how you may pay no more (or possibly even less) to attend a highly-rated private college than your local state university or junior college.

Here's the formula colleges use to determine your need for aid:
need = (cost of attendance) − (merit scholarships/grants) − (expected family contribution)

Assume this middle-class family has an EFC of $10,000 and has assets and income that will not qualify for a Pell grant or other low-income federal/state grants:

Level of School	Sticker Price (cost of attendance)	Scholarships	Aid Granted (up to need)	Out-of-Pocket Costs
Top Private	$55,000	$25,000	$20,000	$10,000
State U	$30,000	$10,000	$10,000	$10,000
Local Jr. College	$15,000	$2,500	$0	$12,500

In this example, our student would pay more to attend the $15,000 local junior college than a $55,000 private college or the $30,000 state university. Here's why: The better endowed a college, the more scholarship dollars they can offer top students. Some of our best, most competitive universities have their entire student body's tuitions paid with a combination of scholarships and/or aid grants.

Another factor I want to re-emphasize is the fact that graduating in four (rather than five, six, or seven years) may be more important than the cost of tuition alone. Consider nursing student A who pays $20,000 a year and graduates on time in four years vs. nursing student B who pays half that, or only $10,000, at a larger state school, but takes five years to graduate. Taking additional years is not unusual because of the crowded upper-level classes in the last two years at large state universities where many junior college students go to finish. At first glance, student B is still clearly better off, having paid $50,000 over five years rather than the $80,000 in student A's more expensive school over four years. But what does the nursing student who graduates in four years do while that fifth-year student is still in school? They are working, making about $50,000. When all five years are considered, what first appeared to be a $30,000 advantage in lower tuition payments for student B turns out to be a $20,000 advantage to student A, even though student A graduated from the more expensive school.

Mistake #3: You pick the wrong college with a focus on cost, not on your student

Based on what I explained earlier, you now know there are some top-ranked schools that have the ability and willingness to give more in aid to meet your EFC. So, without fear of sticker shock, focus on the needs of your student, and go to this site: https://student.collegeboard.org. Type in the names of colleges that best meet your student's needs, and select the "at a glance" section on the left side. Under "quick facts," you will have access to five very important college considerations:

1. The percentage of students who graduate within six years. The higher percentage, the better, even though you want your student to graduate within four years.
2. Under the "average financial aid package," you'll find the average percentage of financial aid met, the tuition, and the fee sticker price. For instance, if you enter Princeton, you will see students have 100 percent of their need met.
3. An idea of whether you may be in their academic scholarship pool. By clicking on the "net price calculator" and providing the requested information, you will know if that school will be more or less likely to meet your need, and how hard you will have to work to keep an academic scholarship while there.
4. The size of the school and its ratio of faculty to students. This may be especially important if your student needs help discovering their major or how best to apply their talents and interest in a career. They will get advice from someone…do you want it to be a professor or a roommate who took a class last semester?
5. If the school meets your expectations for your major. For instance, if your student wants to pursue Electrical Engineering, does the college have a respected Electrical Engineering De-

partment and major, or just some general engineering classes? If you're not sure, click two lines below the "at a glance" section to view "majors and learning environment."

There are many more factors to evaluate other than cost. Those other factors may have a direct impact on how your student performs, the experiences they have, who they meet, the time to graduate, the quality of their chosen degree, and the value of their education. Visit schools to both solidify these factors and narrow your list to six or fewer colleges before you apply. And make sure you know and meet the deadlines for the colleges you are interested in.

Few high school counselors can meet the many advisory needs of their college-bound seniors, and those who do are too often underappreciated. Some of the best I've known have gone into business as independent education consultants. They can help you focus on the important factors for your student, recommend great school matches, keep you appraised of deadlines, and organize FAFSA and college applications. As with most professions, the fees you pay a good advisor will be more than covered by what they save you in time, mistakes, frustration, and cost.

Mistake #4: You waited too long to save, trusted government programs over proven savings vehicles, or relied on financial professionals who offered plans based on assumptions rather than guarantees.

Rather than lament the realities of how college, federal, and state aid funding works, let's concentrate on how we can best position ourselves to be beneficiaries rather than victims. Want to know why the cost of college is going up far faster than inflation and why colleges seem to be able to raise their tuition at will? The short answer is because they can. There is a flood of money available through government programs and loans. It has never been easier for families to go into massive debt for college. It's another bubble, created by willing partners in education, government, banking, and, of course, our political leaders. Families wanting college funding are a large and willing constituency for government programs. Congress will also take dubious credit for special savings programs touted to help families save for college. But the biggest fans of those programs are financial planners who lock up your savings in market-based, "tax-privileged" accounts—like Coverdells, 529-qualified tuition plans, and UGMAS/UTMAS—and then collect their fees for doing so. Even CPAs are often confused with how these plans work with educational tax credits and EFC calculations.

And now that banks have this new boon of college loans that can never be cancelled in bankruptcy and can even be collected by the IRS for delinquency, the government has become an even better banking partner for colleges.

Prosperity economics advisors don't like giving away control of our assets, so prepaids, UTMAS, and UGMAS are not recommended. Coverdells and 529 Plans have market risks, limitations on how much can be saved, and how they're used—not to mention the rules can change with the political winds. In the last market meltdown, stocks and bonds both had huge losses. Even in the best-case scenario, if your timing is right and the stocks and bonds in your Coverdell or 529 Plan meet or exceed the assumptions of our financial planners, the assets still count against your financial need, though at a reduced "parent" level, according to the FAFSA and CSS Profile. Banks provide safety, but certainly not the growth we need to keep up with inflation, let alone college tuition. These are the savings vehicles offered by typical financial planners and advertised on government, mutual fund, and banking websites for college saving. If only there were another choice.

There is. I discovered it after seeing it used by many wealthy families, and you will be surprised by how it meets and exceeds your needs for safe, long-term saving for college and beyond.

A specially designed whole life insurance policy from a dividend-paying mutual insurance company will meet our college savings needs without market risk, provide liquid funds outside the FAFSA or CSS Profile purview, protect those savings from litigation, and, as an added benefit, provide the peace of mind and assurance of college funds. Even in this low-interest rate environment, you can expect an internal rate of return of 4 to 5 percent, with no down years. The dividend rate rises with inflation, historically offers 2 percent over bank CD rates, and can compete with a mutual fund advertising an "average" 12 percent return. I know this seems impossible, but there's an advantage of consistent returns against the ups and downs of market-based investments, and we can prove it.

Through tax-free policy loans, you can pay for college or any other large expense. The accumulation of cash value inside the policy gives you the ability to become your own family bank, following the same wealth-building strategies of some of the richest families in the world. We design our policies to build cash value and use policy riders to add more cash without adding more commissions or fees, making this flexible savings vehicle one of the most economical options available. It is a paradigm shift to see something that is usually considered a cost—and normally valued for just its death benefit—become a savings platform that provides a competitive return (and so many other living, trust-like benefits) at a cost less than a typical mutual fund. And these policies have safely performed through deflation, inflation, depressions, financial crises, and every war for over 100 years.

A prosperity economics advisor can show you how to use a specially designed whole life policy to save for college funding and create a financial engine for your family to provide generational wealth, assurance rather than assumptions, and peace of mind. One way to pay tuition may be to just borrow from the mutual insurance company against the policy's cash value for college and then use prosperity economics guidelines to pay back your family bank at your own pace. No credit checks, no paperwork, just a call to the mutual insurance company to get your cash within a week. By keeping your dollars moving, doing many jobs rather than just one, your focus is on cash flow, not net worth.

Another tactic may be to borrow against some of your policy's cash value to put a down payment on an investment house near the college, which could, in turn, provide rent and cash flow to pay for tuition. This is an example of using your cash value for other investments that will generate the needed cash flow to do other jobs.

Finally, unlike a single purpose account like an IRA or 529 Plan, a properly designed whole life policy creates a tool that has the flexibility to meet many purposes like retirement, emergency funds, education, car purchases, starting a business, investments, and any number of other opportunities. A whole life policy can multiply the things you do with your cash—all in one dynamic, safe, flexible, private account.

I hope this chapter has given you some insights and tools to use toward your college planning. I pray the time you spend together with your student to consider some of the points I've covered in this chapter brings you closer and that you feel confidence, joy, and gratitude as you discover that perfect time and place.

For your convenience, on the next page is a table showing the comparative features and benefits of the plans discussed in this chapter.

	529 College Plans	UGMA/UTMA	Coverdell	Whole Life
TAX ADVANTAGES				
Any earnings grow tax-deferred	▲		▲	▲
Distributions are federal income tax-free	▲		▲	▲
Gift and estate tax benefits	▲	▲		▲
CONTRIBUTION DETAILS				
No contribution maximum		▲		▲
No impact on financial aid				▲
Qualified withdrawals not limited to education expenses		▲		▲
Contributions not limited by the income of the account owner	▲	▲		▲
ACCOUNT MANAGEMENT				
Beneficiary can be changed	▲		▲	▲
Account owner maintains control over distribution of assets	▲		▲	▲
No age limit for the beneficiary (child)	▲			▲
ACCOUNT ATTRIBUTES				
Guaranteed returns not tied to market timing				▲
Loan provisions available for any use at any tiime				▲
Death benefit to pay for college in worst-case scenario				▲
Possible higher returns with market risk	▲	▲	▲	▽
Unspent savings can be repurposed for retirement				▲
Professional management with low fees and commissions	▲	▲	▲	▲
Fees do not increase as account grows over time				▲
Assets protected from litigation				▲

▽ UIL Policies (normally not recommended)

About the Author

As an Air Force Academy graduate, decorated pilot, embassy diplomat, college professor, director of university admissions, adventurer, and truth seeker, John Householder's life passion has always been serving others. His financial advisory firm, Truth Prosperity, always puts its clients first, and John's Series 65 licensing mandates the same.

Mentored by Partners for Prosperity founder Kim Butler and trained by the creator of Truth Concepts Software, Todd Langford, John is proud to serve others in a fiduciary capacity as they seek honest answers to their most pressing financial questions. Like John, Truth Prosperity seeks out the path less traveled.

John enjoys his home life in Fort Worth, Texas, with his wife, Darlene, and two sons, Ethan and Jaron. He can be reached at j.householder@tcu.edu.

Will Duffy, ChFC

Chapter 8

The Other Side of the Coin: Compound Interest—Financial Truths to Protect Your Wealth

Why do we invest our money? Because we want that money to grow. And why do we want our money to grow? Because we'll have more money! It's a simple concept. Money locked in a safe or stashed under a mattress will never grow into more. But when that money is invested, we have the possibility of multiplying those dollars.

This is such a simple concept. But does the average saver and investor really understand the ins and outs of growing their money? To find the answer, let's start with some familiar information. We've all heard about the power of compound interest.

We may have been told that compound interest is magic. Someone may have called it a miracle. It's reported that Albert Einstein referred to compound interest as "the eighth wonder of the world." Einstein felt so strongly about the power of compound interest, he's claimed to have said, "He who understands it, earns it . . . he who doesn't . . . pays it."

With that in mind, join me in learning financial truths about compound interest. You won't need to be an Einstein to understand them—or profit from them.

The Power of Compound Interest

Compound interest sure sounds like a great thing. But let's take it a bit further. Some of this information will probably be familiar. Even if the examples you've heard are slightly different from the ones I'll share here, the concept remains the same.

To demonstrate the power of compound interest, consider this mental experiment: You get to choose whether to receive $1 million today or one penny that's doubled every day for the next 30 days.

Which would you choose? Almost everyone is quick to choose the million dollars. A bird in the hand is worth two in the bush.

Because you are the inquisitive type (after all, you're reading this book), you might ask for more information before you make your choice. You might want to know what a single penny has grown to after one week. The answer is a whopping 64 cents.

You might further ask what the penny has grown to after two weeks. It's a lot more than just 64 cents. The penny, doubled every day, has now grown to $81.92.

Not to push your luck too far, you decide to ask one more question to guide you to making the right decision. Your final question is how much the doubled penny is worth after three weeks. The answer is $10,485.76.

That's still a far cry from the million dollars. So with confidence, you decide you'll take the million dollars—after obtaining what you feel is enough information to make an informed choice.

So what was the right choice? The million dollars—or the penny doubled for 30 days? I'm sure you've already figured out that the penny is the correct answer. You're right. While this is shocking to most, the most shocking part is how much that penny has grown by day 30.

Are you sitting down? A penny doubled every day for 30 days

would grow to more than $5 million! ($5,368,709.12, in fact.) If you don't believe me, grab your calculator and come back to the book in five minutes.

The number is astounding. Unfortunately, investing a penny that will double every day for 30 days is not something we can do. But there's a lesson here. That lesson is the power, magic, and miracle of compound interest.

No matter what we decide to call it, let's be honest. There isn't any magic involved. And this is definitely not a miracle. So what's the secret?

The secret, if you will, lies in the definition of compound interest. The most basic definition of compound interest is when you earn interest on both your principal and your interest. This is different from simple interest, where interest is earned only on the principal. When interest is earned on both principal and interest, big things happen. There is a snowball effect that results in big gains over time as both your principal and your earned interest combine.

FINANCIAL TRUTH #1: COMPOUND INTEREST IS ONE OF THE GREATEST TOOLS FOR BUILDING WEALTH

What does the snowball effect of compound interest mean for you? If you have ever entered into an investment, you probably were shown some numbers to help you picture what your investment might look like at a given time in the future.

These numbers may have been in the form of a prospectus, an illustration, or just a projection on a spreadsheet. You may have done some calculating yourself because it's fun to see what the fruits of our labor could produce one day. These figures demonstrate compound interest.

If you have $100,000 to invest, you might be shown that $100,000 invested for 30 years at 8 percent annual interest will grow to over $1 million ($1,006,265.69 to be exact). Or maybe you want to start contributing to your company's retirement plan, and you decide you would like to contribute $10,000 every year to the plan. That $10,000 contributed annually for 30 years at 8 percent annual interest would also grow to over $1 million. (That's $1,223,458.68 for the detailed folks like myself.) Sounds like a no-brainer. But is it?

Unfortunately, many factors over 30 years will get between us and that million dollars. While these numbers are mathematically correct, they are only part of the truth.

Are you OK with that? Or do you want the whole truth? I passionately believe everyone deserves to know the whole truth about how wealth really works. That is why my company is called Verity Financial, because verity means truth. So as broadcaster Paul Harvey would say, let's look at the rest of the story.

The biggest truth we are never told is that to achieve the true power of compound interest, nothing can be allowed to interrupt the growth. And I mean nothing. As soon as there's an interruption, even a small one, all bets are off. The results are dramatically different.

What kind of interruptions am I talking about? Let me give you a few of the many possible examples. These include investment losses, account fees, taxes on gains, and purchases made with the invested money.

- Investment losses: This is simply when your asset declines in value. A stock you own might drop in price and even be worth less than you paid for it.
- Account fees: These are costs associated with investing. You might have to pay a mutual fund fee if you are invested in a particular fund. Or there could be a fee for management that an advisor charges to manage your accounts.
- Taxes on gains: A tax is something the government assesses to

your investment gains. This could be a capital gains tax associated with a long-term gain in your investment.
- Purchases made with invested money: Finally, you may liquidate all or part of your investment to make a purchase. This could be almost anything, but common large purchases include buying a car, putting a down payment on a house, or responding to a financial emergency.

What's Possible?

Before we look at the impact that interruptions can have on the compound growth of our money, let me ask you a question: Do you think it's possible to earn uninterrupted compound growth? Is it possible to never have any interruptions?

The answer is probably no. And if we cannot earn compound interest without any type of interruption, does that mean all the projections we've looked at are invalid? The answer is probably yes.

A picture is worth a thousand words, so in Figure 8.1, you'll find a representation of what the compound interest curve looks

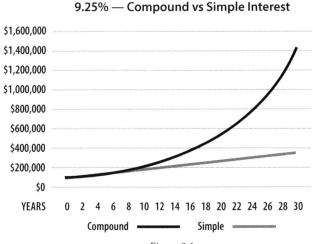

Figure 8.1

like. For comparison's sake, the graph also includes simple interest. The first thing you may notice is that the compound interest curve is not linear, meaning it's not a straight line. The simple interest line, however, is. At first, the two lines are close. But after a few years, the compound interest curve takes off. With time, the real magic happens. (All graphs in this chapter start with $100,000 and have no additional contributions.)

The Effect of Investment Losses

What happens when something interrupts this curve? Let's start by looking at losses. Losses are something most people expect to have occasionally in their investments. For illustration purposes, I cherry-picked a time when the stock market averaged a rate of return of approximately 9 percent. I chose the S&P 500 (including dividends), from 1997 to 2015. This is a period of 19 years when this index averaged a gain of 9.25 percent. Not bad!

Let's start by calculating the results of $100,000 invested for 19 years at a true uninterrupted compound interest rate of 9.25 percent. The account balance at the end of 19 years, as shown in Figure 8.2, would be $537,041.

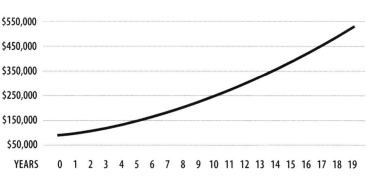

Figure 8.2

As you can see, if we deposited $100,000 into an account and it grew by a compounded 9.25 percent every year, at the end of 19 years, we would have $540,000. That's more than half a million dollars! Surely we would end up with the same dollar figure if we invested in the stock market, if the market returned an average of 9.25 percent over 19 years, right? Let's take a look.

If we had invested $100,000 into the S&P 500 and let it grow from 1997 to 2015, averaging a 9.25 percent return over those 19 years, as shown in Figure 8.3, our balance at the end of the 19 years would be just $392,307. That puts us almost $145,000 short of our $540,000 goal.

How can that be? All the variables were the same: the deposit amount, the 19-year time span, and the 9.25 percent rate of return. So what gives?

There is one key difference between the two scenarios, and that is losses. In the first example, there was never a loss. For 19 years straight, the return was a consistent, positive 9.25 percent. But in the stock market example, there were four years of losses during the 19-year period. These interrupted our compound interest curve.

When we experience a loss, we lose our momentum. And

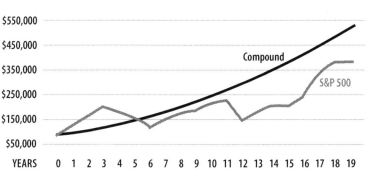

Figure 8.3

when we lose our momentum, we must work to get back to where we were before we can continue to make any progress. Our snowball loses a chunk of snow and has to gather new snow just to regain the missing piece. Let that picture sink in for a moment. Not until the snowball replaces the missing snow can it get back to where it was and start to grow again.

FINANCIAL TRUTH #2: COMPOUND INTEREST STOPS COMPOUNDING WHEN A LOSS IS EXPERIENCED

I want to make sure we are all on the same page. Though in our S&P scenario there were four losses in the 19-year period, the entire period still averaged 9.25 percent. Six of the 19 years had returns of over 20 percent. And two of those six years had a return of over 30 percent!

We are often told that to achieve big gains, we need to expose ourselves to losses. But is that true? Ask yourself one question: With what we've covered so far, would you rather receive a consistent 9.25 percent each year? Or would you prefer to experience some losses for the ability to occasionally experience returns as high as 20 percent and even 30 percent?

I bet you $145,000 that I know which one you would pick now!

A popular children's story beautifully demonstrates what is going on here. It's one of Aesop's fables called "The Tortoise and the Hare." We all remember this classic tale. A tortoise, tired of a hare's boasting, challenges him to a race. What chance does a turtle have? The hare, confident in his ability to win, leaves the tortoise in the dust. He gains such a lead that he decides it's OK to take a nap midway since he cannot lose.

Meanwhile, the tortoise starts the race and continues at the same steady pace. He is consistent. He does not stop or slow down. When the hare awakes, he hears cheers from the finish line celebrating the tortoise's victory. Slow and steady wins the race.

Does this translate to investing? Absolutely. Consistent returns can win the race over the up and down returns of traditional financial thinking.

The bottom line is this: If you do not receive consistent, positive returns in your account, you will not end up with the same amount of money a compound interest calculation says you will. Even if you average the same rate of return that the compound interest calculator used to calculate your growth, you will end up with less money.

Let's look at this from a different perspective. You would have to earn only 7.46 percent interest consistently on your $100,000 for 19 years to end up with the same $390,000 that resulted from being invested in the stock market from 1997 to 2015. That means you lost almost two percentage points from your return—just by adding losses into the mix.

Remember, average returns are not the same as actual returns. (Refer back to pages 4 and 5 for more on this.) An average return is just a number. It cannot tell you how much money you actually have. Only an actual return, one calculated based on actual performance, is an accurate representation of how well your investment did. And as you've just witnessed, the actual return of an average of positive and negative numbers (i.e. ups and downs of the market) will always be less than the average return.

For more financial truths, please see the first book in my The Other Side of the Coin series: *Compound Interest—10 Financial Truths to Protect Your Wealth.*

About the Author

Will Duffy became a millionaire at age 33 by following the same contrarian wealth-building and tax-saving strategies he teaches his clients. He's the author of the industry-rattling book series The Other Side of the Coin,™ which includes the eye-opening Compound Interest: 10 Financial Truths to Protect Your Wealth. *He has earned high praise from legends such as IRA expert Ed Slott, who wrote that book's foreword.*

After attending The Ohio State University and receiving his Chartered Financial Consultant designation from The American College of Financial Services, Will dedicated his work to countering the lies, half-truths, and faulty math that prevent millions of people from realizing their wealth potential.

Will spends every spare moment he can with his wife and four kids, somewhere in the hills and evergreens near Denver, Colorado. He can be reached at Will.Duffy@Verity.Financial.

About the Prosperity Economics Movement

Before the rise of qualified retirement plans, the ever-present 401(k), and the financial planning industry, people built wealth with diligence and common-sense strategies. Investors created wealth through building equity and ownership in properties, businesses, and participating (dividend-paying) whole life insurance. Only a few dabbled in Wall Street stocks, or built "portfolios" on paper.

Wealthy people, in fact, have never stopped practicing what we call "Prosperity Economics."

Today, the common investor is steered away from traditional wealth-building methods. Instead, they are confronted with a confusing labyrinth of funds, rates and complex financial instruments of questionable value. Mutual funds have become so complex that even the people who sell them can't explain them, nor predict when investors are about to lose money. Worse yet, over 30 percent of the average investor's wealth is drained away in fees to a financial industry rife with conflicts of interest.

Prosperity Economics Movement (PEM) is a rediscovery of the traditional simple and trusted ways to grow and protect your money. It was started to provide American investors an alternative to "typical" financial planning, showing us how to control our own wealth instead of delegating our financial futures to corporations and the government.

In Prosperity Economics, wealth isn't measured by how much money you have, but by how much *freedom* you have with your money. The focus is on cash flow rather than net worth. Liquidity, control, and safety are valued over uncertain hopes of a high rate of return. (See the diagram on the next page for some key differences between Prosperity Economics and "typical" financial planning.)

Prosperity Economics Movement is actually comprised of smaller movements that represent alternatives to a financial planning industry we believe has gone off course. You may have heard of The Infinite Banking Concept, Private or Family Banking, Rich Dad Strategies, Circle of Wealth, or Bank on Yourself. Advisors and agents within the movement may use different language and even suggest different financial strategies, but they honor a common set of principles, such as the 7 Principles of Prosperity articulated by Kim Butler.

Typical financial planning is better than nothing, and will get you partway up the hill, but we want to show you how to reach the "peaks" of prosperity. Prosperity Economics shows you how to grow your wealth safely and reliably, with maximum financial flexibility and cash flow. To find out more about Prosperity Economics and PEM, we invite you to explore our website at ProsperityPeaks.com.

Financial Planning vs.	Prosperity Economics™
Meets needs and goals only	Pursues wants and dreams
Minimizes requirements	Optimizes opportunities
Product oriented (only what you buy)	Strategy oriented (what you do)
Rate of return focused	Opportunity cost recovery focused
Institutions control your money	You control your money
Micro (vacuum) based	Macro (big picture) based
Net worth is measurement	Cash flow is measurement
Retirement oriented	Abundant/Freedom oriented
Lives only on interest	Spends and replaces principle
Money stays still	Money moves
Dollars do only one job	Dollars do many jobs
Professional planner is the expert	You are empowered

Consulting a Prosperity Economics Advisor

To explore alternative financial strategies that put you in the driver's seat, we invite you to have a no-cost, no-obligation conversation with a Prosperity Economics Advisor. If you felt like one of the chapters in this book truly connected with you, then we encourage you to contact that author to start the conversation. (Their contact info is at the end of their bio.) If you're not sure which author to contact or have another topic you're curious about, simply email Welcome@ProsperityPeaks.com and we will connect you with a recommended advisor for your situation.

Either way, we will talk with you more about your circumstances and goals—then evaluate how your money might work harder without subjecting it to risk, unnecessary taxation, and never-ending fees. We'll likely suggest proven alternative approaches to "financial planning as usual," and we can even refer you to a truly effective debt solution if needed. We have found these strategies through experience, and they have worked well for our clients.

The three main areas of interest for most people are: cash storage, asset growth, and income. We help clients implement alternative strategies for each of these desires. Our cash strategy grows cash many times faster than typical bank CD rates, while deferring taxes and offering other benefits. Our stock market alternative (especially effective for accredited investors) has an excellent track record with our clients and is not affected by stock market conditions, interest rates, or politics. We can even suggest alternatives to bonds or annuities for cash flow that offer more attractive rates without requiring a long-term surrender of assets.

Again, just contact one of the authors in this book or send an email to Welcome@ProsperityPeaks.com to get started or find out more.

In the meantime, we invite you to explore ProsperityPeaks.com, our website dedicated to Prosperity Economics. And as special thank-you for purchasing this book, you can download our free 60-page ebook, *Financial Planning Has FAILED*. In this landmark work of thought leadership, Kim Butler and Kate Phillips tell it like it is—exposing the truth about the financial industry and illustrating how Prosperity Economics provides real solutions for anyone who wishes to build wealth without Wall Street risks and worries.

Go to ProsperityPeaks.com/Financial and get your copy today.

Book a Prosperity Economics Speaker for Your Next Event

For general audiences

The authors in this book, as well as other Prosperity Economics advisors, are available to speak about the differences between typical financial planning and Prosperity Economics. No matter where your next event will take place, we can connect you with the right expert to talk about any of the following topics and more:
- Retirement plan realities—why qualified plans don't perform as illustrated
- How to save without the risks and roller coaster of the stock market
- Qualified plan alternatives that can significantly reduce future taxes
- The impact of inflation and the danger of retiring too soon
- Saving enough? Why most of us need to save more!
- Financial Planning versus Prosperity Economics

For financial advisors

Author **Kim Butler** and Truth Concepts founder **Todd Langford** are available to speak to advisors or agents about Prosperity Economics, including a Truth Concepts demo that uses calculators and tools to illustrate some of the distinctions of Prosperity Economics. (Truth Concepts is financial software dedicated to telling the whole truth about money. It's built for advisors yet available to anyone at TruthConcepts.com.)

This 2-3 hour presentation is a fascinating eye-opener about various financial philosophies and concepts, and how to talk about and illustrate various financial strategies with clients. Contact Kim@Partners4Prosperity.com for details.

Truth Training

Langford and Butler also conduct seminars several times a year for advisors (anyone is welcome) on using Truth Concepts software. Purchase of the software is not necessary, any advisor can benefit, and some find it so beneficial they return again and again! For more information, go to TruthConcepts.com.

SUMMARY OF THE 7 PRINCIPLES OF PROSPERITY™

1. THINK — Owning a Prosperity mindset eliminates Poverty; scarcity thinking keeps you stuck.

2. SEE — Increase your Prosperity by adopting a macro-economic point of view—a perspective in which you can see how each one of your economic decisions affects all the others. Avoid micro-economic "tunnel vision."

3. MEASURE — Awareness and measurement of opportunity costs enables you to recover them. Ignore this at your peril.

4. FLOW — The true measure of Prosperity is cashflow. Don't focus on net worth alone.

5. CONTROL — Those with the gold make the rules; stay in control of your money rather than relinquishing control to others.

6. MOVE — The velocity of money is the movement of dollars through assets. Movement accelerates Prosperity; accumulation slows it down. Avoid accumulation.

7. MULTIPLY — Prosperity comes readily when your money "multiplies"—meaning that one dollar does many jobs. Your money is disabled when each dollar performs only one or two jobs.

Source: *Busting the Financial Planning Lies: Learn to Use Prosperity Economics to Build Sustainable Wealth* • Copyright © 2012 Prosperity Economics Movement
www.ProsperityPeaks.com

The Prosperity Economics Movement is a not-for-profit organization comprising financial experts who practice Prosperity Economics and individuals who would like to learn how to apply the principles of Prosperity Economics to improve their lives. This book is part of a growing body of information that will support the organization and its members. To learn more or buy your own copy of this book, go to:

www.ProsperityPeaks.com

Made in the USA
Lexington, KY
07 July 2019